The Diaries of
Walter Murray Gibson
1886, 1887

The Diaries of Walter Murray Gibson
1886, 1887

Edited with Introduction and Notes by

Jacob Adler
and
Gwynn Barrett

The University Press of Hawaii 🙢 1973

Copyright © 1973 by The University Press of Hawaii
All rights reserved
Library of Congress Catalog Card Number 75–188977
ISBN 0–8248–0211–X
Manufactured in the United States of America
Designed by Dave Comstock

Contents

———⟨⟩———

Preface

WALTER MURRAY GIBSON's diaries for 1886 and 1887 throw much light on his complex character and on the last few years of his life. As Hawaii's prime minister, was he King Kalakaua's evil angel or was he a statesman of vision? Beyond question he remains one of the most controversial persons in Hawaiian history.

In his diaries we get a personal view of Gibson that is nowhere else to be had. He was, to be sure, an inveterate scribbler, but he was usually somewhat reticent about his own life. Here he writes of his relationships with Kalakaua, and with such notables as Claus Spreckels, the financial angel of the kingdom, and Lorrin A. Thurston, a leader in the revolution of 1887 and one of Gibson's most persistent detractors. We see Gibson blundering as he tries to advance Hawaii's "Primacy of the Pacific" policy by sending Hawaii's one-ship navy to Samoa. We see him overthrown in the revolution of 1887 and exiled to San Francisco.

The diaries tell of his devotion to his daughter and grandchildren. They tell, above all, of his unrequited love for Mother Marianne, who ministered to the lepers at Kakaako and Molokai. She returns respect and admiration for him, but not love. We also see Gibson entangled in a breach of promise suit with a Mrs. St. Clair. He cannot properly defend himself against the suit because he has been exiled and is in failing health.

Since the diaries cover only a two-year period of Gibson's life, the editors have given some background on his earlier years. Obviously, the diaries were not written for publication, so some of the entries are fragmentary and obscure. The editors have therefore provided full notes and have identified all important persons.

⤳§PREFACE§⤳

These diaries are now at Brigham Young University library, Provo, Utah.

Several years ago Rachel Wescoatt, Gibson's granddaughter, lent six diaries (presumably for the years 1882 through 1887) to Kathleen D. Mellen, author of *An Island Kingdom Passes*, a book sympathetic to Gibson. Mrs. Mellen told Gwynn Barrett that after she had the diaries for about three months Mrs. Wescoatt came and destroyed four of them. This took place in Mrs. Mellen's home over her objections. Mrs. Mellen also said that Mrs. Wescoatt told her she could keep the other two diaries. In 1967 Mrs. Mellen gave these to Mr. Barrett with the understanding that they would be taken out of the Hawaiian Islands. Her reason for this, she said, was that certain persons in the Islands had not been sympathetic to Gibson. Later Mrs. Mellen and Mr. Barrett agreed that the diaries would be given to Brigham Young University.

Introduction

A KEY to the complex life and character of Walter Murray Gibson might be found in the tales told him by an uncle who had spent many years in the Far East. When he was about seven, his uncle spoke to him (as Gibson later wrote in *The Prison of Weltevreden*, 1856) "of Sumatra: of the perfumes that wafted from her shores; of the many dainty fruits, and myriad bright-feathered birds of her flowery groves; of the Malay princes." Gibson claimed that his uncle had chosen him to be his heir and partner. "The spirit of adventure, to see strange people and far-off countries, sprang up in me. . . . I felt a longing to go to sea, and to join my uncle." [1]

What little knowledge we have of Gibson's early years comes mainly from his own writings. He claimed that he was born at sea, in the Bay of Biscay. Records of Stamfordham vicarage, Northumberland, England, show that he was baptized on March 9, 1822, at the nearby hamlet of Kearsley. He was the third son of a farm family, John and Lucy Murray Gibson, who emigrated from Northumberland, England, to Montreal, Canada, in the 1830s. About 1837 the family moved to New York City. Walter himself soon moved to South Carolina, after hiring out to drive a carriage from New York City to Pendleton District, S.C.

In the backwoods area of South Carolina, near Sandy Springs, he met Rachel Lewis, the daughter of a planter. She was "a fair gentle girl of my own age [about 15]. . . . We rambled hand in hand to gather wild grapes and the muscadine, then we would rest . . . at the

---

1. Walter M. Gibson, *The Prison of Weltevreden* (New York, 1856), p. 21.

foot of some great tree, and talk of our boyish and girlish fancies; and then without any thought as to mutual tastes, character, or fitness ... but listening only to the music of our young voices; to the alluring notes of surrounding nature; and having only our young faces to admire, we loved; and long ere I was a man, we were married." [2]

His wife died six years later, leaving him a widower with three children, John, Henry, and Talula. Placing them with relatives, he sought adventure but "soon learned that an adventurous spirit, and ambitious hopes, and all lack of training to any labor of the head or hands, were but poor stock in trade among the busy marts of men. ... The drudge and routine of the daily life of trade, soon drove away all dreams of the past. But wealth was eked out of this dull toil," [3] (as a commission agent and manufacturer in New York City).

He traveled in Central America and Mexico, "and then on the road to Acapulco, looked forth toward the Pacific, and thought of early plans of fortune and renown as I looked on the pathway to the East." [4]

On his return to the eastern United States, he bought and fitted out the former U.S. revenue schooner *Flirt*, which he hoped to sell to Guatemala as the nucleus of a navy. Customs officials stopped Gibson from leaving New York City with a cargo of guns. Instead, he set sail in May 1851 for an uncertain destination with a cargo of ice for ballast.

On the way to South America the *Flirt* suffered brawls and mutinies, the chronometer was wrecked, and other navigational aids were lost or stolen. With compass alone to guide his ship, Gibson set out from Brazil, crossed the Atlantic, rounded the Cape of Good Hope, and headed for the East Indian Archipelago. Reaching the Straits of Sunda on Christmas Eve, he sighted the coast of Sumatra. Soon he arrived at Palembang.

The Dutch were wary of non-Dutch foreigners because native Indonesians were restless and reacting against Dutch rule. Gibson wrote a letter on February 4, 1852, to the Sultan of Djambi, who was nominally independent, offering to help him. The Dutch intercepted the letter and charged Gibson with treason.

---

2. *Weltevreden*, pp. 24–25.
3. *Weltevreden*, p. 31.
4. *Weltevreden*, p. 32.

Gibson wrote on February 25 to the governor-general of the Netherlands Indies: "I have allowed . . . my vanity to get the better of my judgment. . . . I remember to have indulged in bravadoes that I would become a potentate in the East . . . but I must ever add in extenuation that this [was] after a plentiful indulgence in wine.

"I have been but too often led away in life by some high-colored romantic idea. . . . I committed grave errors . . . in signing a letter addressed to a native chief in the Malay character, without sufficiently examining . . . its inflammatory contents. . . . I make no defense . . . hoping that there will be found a sufficiency of extenuating circumstances to mitigate the sentence I may strictly deserve." [5]

Through several trials Gibson languished in the prison of Weltevreden at Batavia. Whatever the merits of his case, it became clear that the Dutch intended to make an example of him. He was eventually found guilty of high treason and condemned to twelve years' imprisonment. He did not wait around to hear the sentence. Before it was officially announced, he escaped in April 1853 and boarded a ship for the United States.

He persuaded U.S. Secretary of State William L. Marcy to press a claim against the Dutch for $100,000, for loss of his ship and for false imprisonment. When August Belmont, U.S. chargé d'affaires at The Hague, failed to get prompt action, Gibson persuaded Marcy to let him go to Europe with instructions for Belmont to press the case harder. In September 1854 Belmont wrote the Dutch foreign minister: "It now only remains for my government to take such measures for the enforcement of Mr. Gibson's claim as it may deem fit and proper" [6]—an implied threat of war.

Gibson's actions did not help his case. He seems to have inspired U.S. newspaper attacks on the way Marcy and Belmont handled the case. On a visit to Paris, Gibson attached himself to the U.S. embassy, without authority, to the embarrassment of Ambassador John Y. Mason.

On the way back to the United States, Gibson stopped off at Liverpool, where Nathaniel Hawthorne was U.S. consul. Haw-

---

5. *Executive Document No. 40*, Jan. 20, 1855, U.S. House, 33rd Congress, 2nd sess.

6. Belmont to Van Hall, Sept. 9, 1854. U.S. House, 34th Congress, 1st Sess. Report 307, pp. 130–131.

thorne wrote of him: "A gentleman of refined manners, handsome figure and remarkably intellectual aspect . . . he had so quiet a deportment . . . that you would have fancied him moving always along some peaceful and secluded walk of life."

". . . He had the facility of narrating [his] adventures with wonderful eloquence— . . . in fact, they were so admirably done that I could never more than half believe them. . . . There was an Oriental fragrance breathing through his talk and an odor of the Spice Islands still lingering in his garments." [7]

Gibson also told Hawthorne that at the time of his birth aboard ship another English baby of noble parentage had been born. Having examined certain portraits at an English castle, he had concluded from the resemblance of the portraits to himself that the two babies had been interchanged, and he was really of noble birth. So enchanted was Hawthorne with Gibson's tales that he lent him thirty pounds for his passage home.

Gibson in November 1854 urged upon Marcy that "the United States resort to the only means remaining for enforcing just demands," meaning war. The records were again sent to Congress. When they were printed the Dutch minister to the United States noticed that Gibson's confession of February 25, 1852, was missing, and sent a copy of it to Marcy. Gibson had had access to the file, but it was not established that he had taken the letter. Nevertheless, Marcy no longer supported his claim. For the next few years Gibson kept trying to get action on it, but without result. [8]

As his claim was dying, Gibson got in touch with Dr. J. M. Bernhisel, Mormon delegate to Congress from Utah Territory. The Mormons were having troubles with the United States government, and Gibson proposed a scheme to resettle them on islands in the Pacific. On November 26, 1858, he wrote Bernhisel that he hoped to visit Utah and "accomplish a long cherished purpose of establishing a Colony upon an island of Central Oceanica," [9] even though he

7. Nathaniel Hawthorne, *Our Old Home and English Notebooks* (Boston, 1863), pp. 36–39.

8. On Gibson's Indonesian adventure and claim against the Dutch, see James W. Gould, "The Filibuster of Walter Murray Gibson," in *Hawaiian Historical Society Annual Report for 1959*, pp. 7–32.

9. Gibson to Bernhisel, Nov. 26, 1858, Church of Jesus Christ of Latter-Day Saints' Historian's Office, Salt Lake City, Utah.

did not agree with the Mormon religious views. On May 30, 1859, he wrote Brigham Young, president of the Mormon community at Salt Lake City: "It has been in my heart many years, to propose to you . . . emigration to the islands of Oceanica. . . . I have spent many years among 'the isles that wait' for the Lord; and while I lay in a dungeon in the island of Java, a voice said to me: 'You shall show the way to a people, who shall build up a kingdom in these isles, whose lines of power shall run around the earth.' " [10]

At Salt Lake City a few months later, Young spoke with Gibson and told him to investigate the Mormon faith. If he found it true he could be baptized. He could then go on a mission to the South Seas, and in that way do more good for the islanders than in any other. In January 1860 Gibson was baptized. In April, possibly as a test, he was sent on a mission to the eastern United States. Young wrote of him to William H. Hooper in Washington: "I have invariably found him to be frank, kind hearted, intelligent, upright, and gentlemanly." [11]

Gibson returned to Salt Lake City in November. A few weeks later he left on his Pacific mission, carrying a message of goodwill to the emperor of Japan and the people of Malaya, and holding a general commission as an elder of the Mormon church. He went first to Los Angeles and then by boat to San Francisco, lecturing and visiting with Mormon groups on the way. From San Francisco he left for the Hawaiian Islands, arriving in Honolulu at the end of June 1861.

He gave some well-attended lectures on Malaysia, but did not at first reveal himself to the public as a Mormon. He gave out that he was a traveler intending to stay in the Islands only a few weeks. But soon he found a fruitful field for activity among the Islands' Mormons who had been leaderless since recall of the missionary elders to Utah in 1858 during the troubles with the U.S. government. Gibson showed his official commission, decorated with ribbons and seals, and assumed the title of "Chief President of the Islands of the Sea and of the Hawaiian Islands for the Church of

---

10. Gibson to Young, May 30, 1859, Historian's Office, Salt Lake City, Utah.

11. Young to Hooper, Apr. 26, 1860, Brigham Young Collection, Yale University Library.

the Latter Day Saints." (The title "president" is still used for persons who preside over such church missions.)

He took firm control of mission affairs, and established headquarters on the island of Lanai. He gave new life to the mission, built many new structures on Lanai, planted wheat and cotton, and raised sheep and goats. Among the buildings was a schoolhouse, and Gibson showed much interest in education. He himself quickly learned the Hawaiian language and customs. He was a practical religionist, and felt that among the Hawaiian Mormons there had been too much of prayers and meetings and not enough of work.

Toiling day by day, he still dreamed of an Oceanic empire: "I must not desert the seed I have planted here on the Hawaiian Islands. The seed of Oceanican organization is in Lanai . . . this is the nucleus of development. . . . I set up my standard here and it goes hence to the islands of the sea. Lanai shall be famous in Malaysia, in Oceanica . . . this is but the baby of my kingdom." [12]

Dwight Baldwin, a non-Mormon, wrote of Gibson in his 1863 mission report: "He seems to be engaged mostly in agriculture, raising poultry and sheep and trafficking with the natives. He has leased land of the government . . . and I suspect will soon have the resources of the island under his control." [13] (It should be kept in mind that Gibson was getting no salary or any other material support from Mormon headquarters in Salt Lake City.)

Some of the Hawaiian Mormons became concerned about Gibson's actions. In late 1863 they wrote to some of the elders in Utah to express their doubts and fears. Brigham Young appointed an investigating committee of elders and apostles to go to the Islands. They found that Gibson was preaching false doctrine and questioned his willingness to submit to the authority of the church. They decided in April 1864 to cut Gibson off from the church, a decision later confirmed in Utah.

Most of the Mormons left Lanai. A few years later many of them went to newly established headquarters at Laie, Oahu. Gibson stayed on Lanai, refused to give up title to his lands, and developed them mainly as a sheep ranch. (Young himself did not consider the land matter an important point in the excommunication.)

---

12. Diary, Jan. 31, 1862. Typed copy in Archives of Hawaii.
13. Cited in K. P. Emory, *The Island of Lanai* (Honolulu: Bishop Museum, 1924; reprinted, 1969), p. 9.

May it please Your Excellency,

          I once more take the liberty of
addressing you in relation to my case; - and
I now desire to do so, without any feeling of
attempt at defence; but rather to throw
myself wholly upon Your Excellency's
clemency; and that of your government.
    I am at the moment, at liberty; but ex-
pecting incarceration at any time, I must
say, that I feel this state of uncertainty
to be a severe punishment. - I know, and
avow most regretfully, that I have allowed
my fancy and my vanity to get the better
of my judgement, - much of the time, during
my stay within the jurisdiction of the Netherlands Indian government - I remember
to have indulged in bravadoes, that I would
become a potentate in the East; - and this
to Europeans and Natives, who I cannot
suppose attached any more importance to

238

what I said, than as a vainglorious boast;-
but I must ever add in extenuation, that
this after a plentiful indulgement in wine -
I have been but too often, led away in
life, by some high coloured romantic
idea :- But as I said at the commencement, I write not for defence on this oc-
casion;- but to avow, that I committed
grave errors in a too free way of speaking
with natives, and ultimately in allowing
my mate to depart into the interior, and in
signing a letter addressed to a native
chief in the Malay Character, without sufficiently examining or endeavoring to know
its inflammatory contents - I acknowledge
the serious fault of sending a communi-
cation of whatever nature to such a person-
age; and allowing the mate of my vessel,
to leave ti penetrate into the interior without acquainting the authorities - I cannot
remember more particulars, than I have all-
ready given in previous statements;- and
I now crave Your Excellency's consideration

of all the facts, and then dispose of
me as your leniency shall dictate —
I make no defense; but only pray
for a speedy judgment; — hoping that
there will be found a sufficiency of extenuating circumstances to mitigate the
sentence I may strictly deserve —

I remain

Your Excellency's

Most obedt. Servt.

Walter M. Gibson

Batavia, Feb. 25th 1852.

Gibson to Governor General of Netherlands East Indies, Batavia, February 25, 1852. One of the most important documents introduced at Gibson's trial for high treason against the Dutch. *Algemeen Rijksarchief, Depot Schaarsbergen, The Netherlands*

Walter Murray Gibson. *Archives of Hawaii*

In 1868 Gibson publicly concerned himself with Hawaii's pressing labor and population problems. He proposed that the Hawaiian government bring in from Malaysia races "cognate" with the Hawaiian. To further such immigration, Kamehameha V commissioned him as "commercial agent to Singapore." Nothing came of this, and he never even got to Singapore; but on a trip to the United States he recruited some thirty Californians for the settlement on Lanai. He proposed to enter into sharecropping arrangements with them. Most of them found Lanai inhospitable, and within a year practically all of them had left. Gibson continued to urge upon the government Malaysian immigration.

Gibson brought himself and his policies to public notice in 1873 by publishing a Hawaiian-English newspaper, the *Nuhou*. He spoke out especially against the proposed cession of Pearl Harbor in return for a possible U.S.-Hawaii reciprocity treaty. (He was not against the treaty itself.) He put himself forward as the friend and champion of the Hawaiian people. The planters and businessmen accused him of cultivating antiforeign sentiment.

Gibson in 1874 urged the election of David Kalakaua to the throne over the dowager Queen Emma. In the campaign for the legislature of 1876, Gibson (not himself a candidate) published in English and Hawaiian an *Address to the Hawaiian People* again urging support of King Kalakaua. He also deprecated agitation against the reciprocity treaty which the king had helped to obtain.

Ranch life on Lanai evidently failed to offer the restless Gibson enough challenge. In 1878 he moved to Lahaina, Maui, and won election to the legislature. He became the leader of the Hawaiian representatives and led the fight for such royal appropriations as that for a new palace. Though firmly supporting the king, Gibson attacked Kalakaua's conservative non-Hawaiian cabinet ministers in a report of the finance committee of which he was chairman. He showed great interest in improving the leper settlement at Molokai. He also headed a committee to prepare instructions for the Hawaiians on health and sanitation. The resulting book on the subject listed Gibson as its author. All this activity made it clear that he was aiming to become one of the king's ministers.

He won a seat in the 1880 legislature by a large majority. He continued to support such royal measures as one for the belated coronation of the king and queen. Foreshadowing the Gibson-Kalakaua policy of "Primacy of the Pacific," Gibson introduced a resolution that Hawaii send a royal commissioner to the peoples of Polynesia. The resolution was adopted but not at once acted upon.

During the campaign for the 1882 legislature, the *Hawaiian Gazette* bitterly attacked Gibson in a series of articles titled "The Shepherd Saint of Lanai." Written in English, the articles and a resulting pamphlet received scant attention from the largely native Hawaiian electorate. Gibson received more votes than any other candidate. British Commissioner James H. Wodehouse wrote the British Foreign Office that Gibson was stirring up the races and that his election might lead to disorder and revolution.

Some members of the Honolulu business-planter establishment offered Gibson support for the premiership for his promise to support renewal of the U.S.-Hawaii reciprocity treaty. He refused, and became premier on his own terms in May 1882. He formed a cabinet that included two Hawaiians and announced a "new departure in Hawaiian politics." U.S. Minister J. M. Comly said the new cabinet was "looked upon with apprehension and dread by the foreigners who do the business and pay the taxes of the country." [14] Commissioner Wodehouse predicted that the whole burden of government would fall on Gibson.

Gibson aligned himself with Claus Spreckels, the sugar king of California and Hawaii, to whom the government had to look for financial support. In the 1882 legislature he backed a measure to give Spreckels 24,000 acres of land on Maui in settlement of a doubtful claim by Spreckels to certain crown lands. Besides this, the legislature was much criticized for extravagance. Appropriations came to almost twice the expected revenues of about two million dollars.

Gibson was one of the main planners of Kalakaua's coronation which took place in February 1883. He proclaimed that Kalakaua was the first Hawaiian king with the brains and heart of a statesman. In further pursuit of Hawaii's "Primacy of the Pacific" policy, Gibson in 1883 drafted an appeal to the great powers to recognize the right of Pacific polynesian communities to self-government, and to "guarantee to them the same favorable opportunities which have made Hawaii prosperous and happy, and which incite her national

---

14. Comly to U.S. Sec. State, June 5, 1882, U.S. Dept. State, Dispatches Hawaii, **XX.**

spirit to lift up a voice among the Nations in behalf of sister islands and groups of Polynesia." [15] This appeal, really a protest, was sent to twenty-six nations. Most of them ignored it.

The planters and businessmen—even though they were prospering and enjoying a light burden of taxation—became more and more dissatisfied with the foreign policy and other policies of the Gibson regime despite certain achievements of the regime which favored that group. In 1885, for example, the government took an important step toward solving Hawaii's labor-population problems by bringing in large numbers of Japanese.

As charges of incompetence and extravagance against the regime continued to be raised there were frequent shakeups in the cabinet. Gibson himself hung on. In May 1885, a group headed by Sanford B. Dole, William R. Castle, and Lorrin A. Thurston coordinated opposition to the regime and campaigned to elect more Independent party candidates to the legislature. At the beginning of 1886 this group was bitterly fighting Gibson; and he was fighting back.

In his early sixties at this time, he was apparently at the height of his political power. But his health was fast failing and though he tried he was really no longer able to carry the burdens of government. In his diaries he has written of the disastrous legislative session of 1886, of his efforts to keep the kingdom financially afloat by steering a course between Spreckels and Kalakaua, and of the disastrous outcome of the "Primacy of the Pacific" policy.

In mid-1887 came a revolution that cost Kalakaua much of his power and drove Gibson out of the kingdom under threat of hanging. He entered a hospital in San Francisco. At the end of the year he wrote in his diary: "The improvement in my health continues." Less than a month later he died.[16]

---

15. Hawaii, *Report of the Minister of Foreign Affairs*, 1884, Appendix.

16. On Gibson's life, generally, see R. S. Kuykendall, *The Hawaiian Kingdom, 1854–1874* (Honolulu: University of Hawaii Press, 1953), especially references on p. 278; R. S. Kuykendall, *The Hawaiian Kingdom, 1874–1893* (Honolulu: University of Hawaii Press, 1967).

For a popular account, see "Gibson, the King's Evil Angel" in James A. Michener and A. Grove Day, *Rascals in Paradise* (New York: Random House, 1957), pp. 112–146; references, p. 357. The account most favorable to Gibson is that by Kathleen D. Mellen, *An Island Kingdom Passes* (New York: Hastings House, 1958). See also Gwynn Barrett, "Walter Murray Gibson: the Shepherd Saint of Lanai Revisited," *Utah Historical Quarterly* (Spring 1972), pp. 142–162.

1886

FRI., JAN. 1 — *Wea. — Fine — Called on Mr and Mrs Merrill, Mr & Mrs Wodehouse, Mr and Mad Feer, Senhr & Mad Canavarro, the Bickertons, Mrs Hendry. At Branch Hospital. A very pleasant hour at the Convent with all the Sisters. Bishop Hermann and Fʳ Clement called at same time at Convent. The Bishop's blessing. M[other Marianne]'s white rose with one drop of blood.*

JAN. 1. *George W. Merrill*, U.S. minister resident.

James H. Wodehouse, British commissioner and consul general.

Henri Feer, French consul and commissioner.

A. de Souza Canavarro, Portuguese consul and commissioner.

Richard F. Bickerton, a judge who later became a justice of the supreme court. He presided at a breach of promise suit brought against Gibson. See diary entry of May 19, 1887.

Mrs. Eugene R. Hendry, assistant principal of Fort Street School.

Branch Hospital, a leper hospital in the Kakaako district, on the waterfront between Waikiki and downtown Honolulu. The *Convent* of St. Francis for the sister-nurses was within the fenced-off hospital complex. Gibson had been largely responsible for persuading the legislature to establish the hospital and had also done much to have the Catholic church send the Sisters of Charity as nurses.

Hermann Koeckemann, bishop of Olba, highest-ranking Catholic in the kingdom.

Father Clement Evrard, an assistant to Bishop Hermann. Father Clement arrived in the Islands in 1864 on the same ship as the leper priest of Molokai, Father Damien.

M[other Marianne]'s white rose. We shall hear more — much more — of Mother Marianne. Also referred to as S.M., M.M., Sr.M.

3

SAT., JAN. 2 — *Called on Mrs Neumann, Mrs Gulick. Tone of health good.*

JAN. 2. *Mrs. Neumann,* wife of Paul Neumann, attorney general.
Mrs. Gulick, wife of Charles T. Gulick, minister of interior.

SUN., JAN. 3 — *Robbery of Post Office. I advised Gulick to place the Gen. P. Office for a time in charge of the Marshal, with Scrymgeour as bookkeeper. Talula & children preparing to go to Lahaina.*

JAN. 3. *Robbery.* One Thomas B. Walker was charged with the robbery and acquitted. There was some suspicion that the robbery was an inside job. *Pacific Commercial Advertiser,* Apr. 9, 1886; *Hawaiian Gazette,* Apr. 13, 20, 1886.

Marshall, John H. Soper.

Allan B. Scrymgeour [Scrimgeour], a former business manager of the *Advertiser.* He became cashier-bookkeeper of the general post office. See McKenney's *Hawaiian Directory* (San Francisco) for 1884, and also for 1888.

Talula . . . to Lahaina. Talula Lucy Gibson Hayselden (1843?–1903), Gibson's only daughter, who was married to Frederick Harrison Hayselden (1851–1924). Gibson owned a home called *Lanikeha* near the Lahaina, Maui, waterfront. Talula obituary, *Pacific Commercial Advertiser,* May 17, 1903; *Paradise of the Pacific,* June 1903, p. 9. F. H. Hayselden obituary, *Honolulu Advertiser,* Jan. 3, 1924; *Honolulu Star-Bulletin,* Jan. 3, 1924.

MON., JAN. 4 — *Wea. — Warm — Political activity. Fred interviewed Bishop H[ermann]. Will instruct as requested. Wm G. I[rwin] will aid $3000. Kaulukou gives me the*

4

situation at Hilo — Hitchcock can & must be beaten. At Br [anch]. H [ospital]. with M.

JAN. 4. *Political activity* refers to campaign for 1886 legislature.

Bishop Hermann will instruct. It is not clear whether this has to do with politics, or with Catholic instruction for Gibson.

Wm. G. Irwin, partner of Claus Spreckels, the sugar king.

John Lot Kaulukou, labor contract agent for island of Hawaii, was elected to the 1886 legislature from the Hilo district. There was no law against officeholders running for the legislature. This was one of the complaints of the Opposition party.

David Howard Hitchcock, a Hilo, Hawaii, lawyer. He was beaten.

TUES., JAN. 5 — *Wea. — Warm — Cecil Brown spending largely at Laie. Have got his operations exactly.* On peut les déjouer. *V. V. Ashford urges the Govt to let his bro. Clarence get in at Waimea, Kauai. Says he turned the Austins of Hilo over to us.*

Talula, Fred & all the children with Lita [?] & Kahaulelio left for Lahaina per Kinau.

JAN. 5. *Cecil Brown*, attorney, candidate from Koolauloa, Oahu. He was one of two Opposition candidates elected to the 1886 legislature.

On peut les déjouer. 'We must outsmart them'.

Volney V. Ashford and his brother *Clarence W.* had a law office in Honolulu. Clarence ran on the Opposition ticket and was defeated. Volney was head of the Honolulu Rifles, a voluntary but semiofficial military company. The

Ashford brothers were born in Canada and educated in the
United States.

Left for Lahaina, Maui. *Lita*(?) and *Kahaulelio* possibly
were servants. Passenger list for the interisland steamer
Kinau shows: "F. H. Hayselden, wife, 5 children, and
servant," only one. *Daily Bulletin,* Jan. 6, 1886.

WED., JAN. 6 — *Wea.* — *Fair & warm* — *A lonely house.*
The band at the Branch Hospital. Mrs Gascoyne called
to look after things in the house. Dictating editorials to
Wright.

JAN. 6. *Gibson's house,* called *Halaaniani* ('waving pandanus'?),
was on King Street, across from Iolani Palace and near the
Hawaiian Opera House or Music Hall.

Mrs. Elizabeth Gascoyne, a dressmaker.

William Horace Wright (1842–1900), clerk in the foreign
office. Besides helping Gibson with editorials, he wrote
reports in the foreign office and other departments. He
celebrated the end of the nineteenth century by committing
suicide. *Pacific Commercial Advertiser,* Jan. 2, 1901;
Evening Bulletin, Jan. 1, 1901.

THURS., JAN. 7 — *Wea.* — *Fair* — *Photos taken at the*
Branch Hospital. Talk of Lahilahi and others in the hospital
yard. Mrs Neumann, Mrs Strong called.
Uncertainty about Molokai. Influence of the Castle,
Thurston raid. Il faut le déjouer.

JAN. 7. *H. W. Lahilahi* was a representative to the 1882
legislature and one of the signers, with Gibson, of an odd

electioneering tract, *Move! Excel the Highest!* (Honolulu, 1882), copy in Archives of Hawaii.

Mrs. Strong, Isobel Osbourne Strong (Mrs. Joseph Dwight Strong), stepdaughter of Robert Louis Stevenson.

Castle, Thurston raid. Thurston claimed that the board of health (of which Gibson was president) had tried to stop him from campaigning among the lepers on Molokai. *Hawaiian Gazette,* Jan. 26, 1886.

The *Advertiser* accused Castle and Thurston of mixing prayers and politics at a Sunday school convention on Molokai. The *Bulletin* claimed that the political meeting had taken place *after* the convention. *Pacific Commercial Advertiser,* Jan. 5, 1886; *Daily Bulletin,* Jan. 6, 1886. Castle was elected in the Wailuku, Maui, district, and Thurston in the Molokai-Lanai district. Thurston's victory was especially galling to Gibson. As president of the board of health, Gibson regarded the Molokai leper settlement as his special preserve; and he owned or leased most of Lanai.

William Richards Castle (1849–1935), born in Honolulu of missionary parents, was attorney general of the kingdom in 1876, and a member of the legislatures of 1878, 1886, 1887, and 1888. He served on the 1893 annexation commission, and in 1895 was minister from the Republic of Hawaii to the United States. *Men of Hawaii* (Honolulu: Star-Bulletin, 1917).

Lorrin A. Thurston (1858–1931), lawyer, editor, member of 1886 legislature, and minister of interior, 1887–1890. He was prominent in the revolutionary movements of 1887 and 1893. *Men of Hawaii* (Honolulu: Star-Bulletin, 1921).

Il faut le déjouer. 'We must outsmart them'.

FRI., JAN. 8 — *Wea. — Beautiful — A strong opposition feeling has been aroused, that is turning the popular current of thought against me. I can correct this.*

Sent to Convent some butter, buttermilk & cakes prepared at the house. A sweet note from M. "Hope [?] Nearing Home."

SAT., JAN. 9 — *The King & Queen returned per* Kinau
10 A.M. I met them on board. Fred returned — left all well
at Lahaina.

The opposition gets fiercer — I am prepared for a blow.
The King buoyant and hopeful.

A pleasant hour at Kakaako. Dr & Mrs Webb called.

JAN. 9. *King Kalakaua & Queen Kapiolani returned.* Earlier in
the day, the Royal Guards and the Royal Band had gone
to meet the wrong ship. "It was deemed best, after this
blunder . . . to receive the party . . . with a truly civic
ovation. . . . A royal salute of seven-second guns was fired
from the battery in honor of the arrival of their Majesties."
Besides going on board the *Kinau,* Gibson accompanied
the royal procession to Iolani Palace. King Kalakaua had
been doing some electioneering on the outer islands. *Daily
Bulletin,* Jan. 9, 1886.

Kakaako. The Kakaako complex included the branch leper
hospital; the Kapiolani Home for girls who were not lepers,
but who were born of leprous parents; and the convent for
the Franciscan sisters.

Dr. E. Cook Webb, a homeopathic physician who came
to Honolulu in May 1880. He had been chief of staff of
the Homeopathic Hospital, Ward Island, N.Y., where
he had a "reputation as a physician and a gentleman!"
Pacific Commercial Advertiser, May 22, 29, 1880.

SUN., JAN. 10 — *Busy with election calls.*
The King at the house after Church at St Andrews. He
spent over an hour with me — very hopeful & buoyant.

JAN. 10. *St. Andrew's Cathedral* (Anglican Episcopal), at
Beretania and Queen Emma streets. It was named for the
saint's feast day on which Kamehameha IV died in 1863.
The chancel was completed for Christmas services in 1886.

Old Honolulu, a Guide to Oahu's Historic Buildings, ed.
Frances Jackson, Agnes Conrad, Nancy Bannick (Honolulu:
Historic Buildings Task Force, 1969), p. 40.

  "Kalakaua . . . at the time of his election as king was one
of the trustees of the Anglican Church in Hawaii. In later
years, his interest in the Church quite disappeared." *The
Episcopal Church in Hawaii* (Honolulu: privately printed,
1952), p. 19.

MON., JAN. 11 — *Very busy all day. Kapena goes per* Kinau
*to visit Lahaina, Hana & other places to straighten up
matters.*

  *Wrote to Talula & Walter. Went to theatre to see Miss
Ward in "Forget me not." Dr and Mrs Webb called.*

JAN. 11. *John M. Kapena* (1843–1887), one of Hawaii's
greatest orators, was near the end of his short, sad life.
He was a member of the house of nobles, 1876–1886.
He served twice as minister of finance, and held many other
offices in the Kalakaua regime. Drink finally worsted him.

Walter Hooulu Hayselden (1876–1949), son of Talula
and Fred. Obituary, *Honolulu Star-Bulletin*, Mar. 29, 1949;
Honolulu Advertiser, Mar. 30, 1949.

Genevieve Ward, of "world-wide reputation," played
Stephanie de Mohrivart, supported by a local cast. At
the Hawaiian Opera House, "every chair was occupied . . .
mainly by the intellect, wealth, and fashion of the city."
Daily Bulletin, Jan. 12, 1886.

TUES., JAN. 12 — *Edith and Harry Turton arrived by the*
St. Paul. *Edith went with Mrs Neumann to her house —
Harry remains here.*

  Called at Kakaako.

JAN. 12. *Edith and Harry Turton*, residents of Lahaina, Maui, were returning from San Francisco. Henry (or Harry) Turton was a retired sugar planter. His daughter Edith was a close friend of Talula Hayselden. See obituary of Henry Turton, *Daily Bulletin*, July 11, 1887.

WED., JAN. 13 — *Health continues good. I attribute some improvement to steady use of buttermilk which is churned at the house.*

THURS., JAN. 14 — *A little bit put out with matters at Br. H.*

FRI., JAN. 15 — *At Br. H. today and all very well.*

SAT., JAN. 16 — *My birthday. Four young ladies spent the day with me — Misses Eva Neumann, Edith Turton, Nellie Brown & Virginia Dillingham. I had minstrel music. The King, the Merrills, Bickerton, Walker, Maggie & Annie, Mrs Hendry and many others at house this evening. Mr Want from the* Alameda. *The King staid up with me till 2 oclock in morning.*

JAN. 16. *My birthday*. Probably Gibson's sixty-fourth, although the newspapers called it his sixty-second.

Eva Neumann, oldest daughter of Paul Neumann, attorney general.

Nellie B. Brown, daughter of Capt. John H. Brown who was an agent of the board of health of which Gibson was the head. On Nov. 17, 1890, she married William C. King. *Hawaiian Gazette*, Nov. 25, 1890. McKenney's *Hawaiian Directory*, 1884 and 1888.

Virginia Dillingham. Possibly a mis-writing of "Virginia Gilliland" (see note for Feb. 6, 1886). No appropriate record has been found of a Virginia Dillingham.

John Smith Walker (1826–1893), born in Aberdeen, Scotland, came to Hawaii in 1854. He was prominent in both business and politics. He was minister of finance, 1874–1876, president of the 1886 legislature, and served in many other governmental positions. Gibson's will named Walker as executor. For obituary, see *Hawaiian Gazette*, May 30, 1893; *Pacific Commercial Advertiser*, May 30, 1893; *Daily Bulletin*, May 29, 1893.

Maggie and Annie, daughters of J. S. Walker.

Randolph C. Want, solicitor general in London for the New South Wales, Australia, government. He was on his way to London as a commissioner to the London Colonial and Indian Exhibition. He had some interest in a scheme for a Pacific cable. *Hawaiian Gazette*, Feb. 2, 1886; *Pacific Commercial Advertiser*, Oct. 26, 1886, citing New Zealand Herald, n.d.

SUN., JAN. 17 — *Went in carriage with flowers of yesterday's festivity to Convent. Took also some cake.*

MON., JAN. 18 — *An interesting talk with the King this morning. An effort made by Bishop & others to reinstate Dr Arning.*
　　At Br. H.

JAN. 18. *Dr. Edward Christian Arning*, dermatologist, venereologist, and bacteriologist, came to Hawaii on Nov. 8, 1883, on the same ship that brought Mother Marianne and six other Franciscan nuns. He had come at Gibson's invitation to help in the battle against leprosy. On his battles against both leprosy and Gibson, see O. A. Bushnell's "Dr. Edward Arning, the First Microbiologist in Hawaii," *Hawaiian Journal of History*, vol. 1, 1967, pp. 3–30.

Charles R. Bishop, Honolulu banker, one of three businessmen to whom nine physicians appealed on Arning's behalf after Gibson had fired him. See Bushnell, "Arning," pp. 20–21.

TUESDAY, JAN. 19 — *Grand requiem Mass at the Catholic Cathedral — I went in full Court uniform. After Mass, called at Br. H. in my uniform.*

Harry & Edith Turton left per Kinau — I sent letters to Talula, Walter & Lucy & box of things.

JAN. 19. *Grand requiem mass* "for the repose of the soul of Don Alfonso XII, late King of Spain." King Kalakaua and practically the entire diplomatic corps in Honolulu attended. *Pacific Commercial Advertiser*, Jan. 20, 1886.

Catholic Cathedral, Our Lady of Peace cathedral, on Fort Street near Beretania. It dates from 1843. *Old Honolulu, a Guide to Oahu's Historic Buildings*, ed. Frances Jackson et al., p. 43.

Lucy, Talula Lucy Gibson Hayselden (1877–1933), daughter of Talula and Fred. Obituary, *Honolulu Advertiser*, May 4, 1933.

WED., JAN. 20 — *Intensity of the canvass. The opposition have, or have had, a fund not less than $30,000, and are spending it judiciously. I am getting off extras and posters for every district in the Kingdom.*

Taking photos at Br Hosp[l]. I spent the aft. there.

THURS., JAN. 21 — *Sent carriage to give Sisters a drive. The Mother & Sr Rosalia at my house.*

An interesting talk with the King. He wants us Ministers to prove our strength in this election. H[is]. M[ajesty]. proposes the removal of Whitney, P.M.G.

JAN. 21. *Sr. Rosalia* McLaughlin, one of the original group of Franciscan sisters who arrived in Honolulu with Mother Marianne on Nov. 8, 1883. L. V. Jacks, *Mother Marianne of Molokai* (New York: Macmillan, 1935), p. 30.

Henry M. Whitney, postmaster general, was also a prominent journalist and editor. He was not removed until mid-April 1886, and soon after that he bought an interest in the *Hawaiian Gazette*. He and Gibson had often been on opposite sides of the editorial fence. An extremely able journalist, Whitney was probably more of a threat to the government outside it than in it. See *Daily Bulletin*, Apr. 15, 1886; *Hawaiian Gazette*, May 25, 1886; *Pacific Commercial Advertiser*, May 26, 1886.

FRI., JAN. 22 — *The King proposes to remove all the officers of the Waterworks and Post Office.*

    Mr Peddie called on me.

    Williams finished some photos of Sisters.

JAN. 22. *Officers of the waterworks.* Gulick, minister of interior, had reported a shortage in the accounts of Charles B. Wilson, superintendent of the waterworks. Cabinet Council Minute Book, Jan. 13, 1886, Archives of Hawaii.

John Dick Peddie, member of British parliament, Kilmarnock burghs, 1880–1885. As a prominent visitor, he had breakfast with the king. Later he visited Kauai with Theo. H. Davies, important Honolulu sugar factor. *Modern English Biography*, ed. Frederic Boase (New York: Barnes & Noble, 1965), vol. 2, p. 1430. *Pacific Commercial Advertiser*, Jan. 21, 23, 1886; *Hawaiian Gazette*, Jan. 26, Feb. 2, 1886.

James J. Williams, one of Honolulu's best-known photographers.

SAT., JAN. 23 — *The birthday of Sr M. Presented a plated service to Convent of St Francis. A pleasant hour with Sr M.*

The King said this evening he did not want a man in office who was opposed to me.

JAN. 23. *Birthday of Sr M[arianne]*. Her forty-eighth according to Gibson's memorandum in this diary (see Memoranda, 1886 Diary). More likely it was her fiftieth. See L. V. Jacks, *Mother Marianne of Molokai*, pp. 190–192.

Presented a plated service. Gibson in 1885 had written Mother Marianne a somewhat romantic explanation of the word *hookupu* 'tribute or ceremonial gift': "It is a custom of the Hawaiian people, when a high chief or chiefess, or any highly esteemed . . . stranger comes to visit them, that they make an offering (hookupu) . . . of some product or creature of the land or water, and of some article of food: — and I conforming to this custom of the land of my adoption offer for the acceptance of the noble ladies of your sisterhood just arrived, who have come to the help of a poor and suffering people, a few flowers from my garden, a turkey from my ranch . . . and some light cakes baked this afternoon by my cook. The hookupu is regarded by Hawaiians as a small heart offering to the noble and most welcome stranger." Apr. 22, 1885, Archives of Franciscan Sisters, Syracuse, N.Y.

SUN., JAN. 24 — *Sent pie and sponge cake to Convent. A nice letter in return.*
Busy with campaign articles in the Hawaiian language.

JAN. 24. *Campaign articles in Hawaiian*. Gibson was fluent in the language. He knew the importance of appealing to the Hawaiians, who comprised the majority of the electorate, in their own language. (See also diary entries of Jan. 29 and 31, 1886.) Some of the articles were placed in the *Elele Poakolu* (Wednesday Messenger) run by Gibson's friend Dan Lyons.

MON., JAN. 25 — *The extradition of McCarthey. Neumann wanted me to act at once. I would not on requisition of Gov of Calif — but got Mr Merrill to request one.*

A happy hour at Br. H. The King & all the candidates at my house.

JAN. 25. *Extradition of John W. McCarthey* [McCarthy], an alleged embezzler from San Francisco, former clerk of the California supreme court. *Pacific Commercial Advertiser*, Feb. 8, 1886. Many items about his extradition and trial appeared in the Honolulu papers.

TUES., JAN. 26 — *The King at my house at 1 P.M. Earnest confidences. The King left per* W. G. Hall *for Kona at 3 P.M.*

Pained to hear that S. M. was very unwell.

JAN. 26. *The king left per W. G. Hall*, an interisland steamer. One purpose of the trip was to do some electioneering for the Government party on the island of Hawaii.

WED., JAN. 27 — *A restless night — unwell all day.*

Sent cooked duck to the Convent. After dark about 7 P.M. I went to Convent to enquire after health of S. M. Happy to meet her, and find her much better.

THURS., JAN. 28 — *My throat troubles me very much — warm southerly weather.*

At Br. H — unusually pleasant. Williams brot photos of Sisters. Called on Dr and Mrs Webb.

FRI., JAN. 29 — Passed a bad night — throat troubled me very much. Drove to Convent at noon. Delivered 2 bots of wine — made no stay.

Working hard on native articles. Striking the opposition at all points.

SAT., JAN. 30 — A good night's rest. Much better this morning.

At Br. H. in the afternoon.

The opposition is manifestly weakened — blunders of Waterhouse. Stinking salmon & pewter half dollar.

JAN. 30. *Stinking salmon & pewter half dollar.* A reference to (unsupported) charges of sharp business practice and bribery on the part of Henry Waterhouse. He was a merchant and a candidate for the Honolulu district. See "Campaign Notes," *Pacific Commercial Advertiser*, Feb. 2, 1886.

SUN., JAN. 31 — Feeling well this morning.

Sent to Convent at noon a chicken pot pie & custard pudding, with note. No reply — disappointed.

Getting ready campaign articles in native daily.

MON., FEB. 1 — Passed an unpleasant night. Feverish and uncomfortable.

At Kakaako 4 P.M. A pleasant hour.

TUES., FEB. 2 — A good night's rest, and all right this morning.

Anxious about the morrow. Our organization of lunas is good and nothing is neglected.

FEB. 2. *Luna* ('high' in Hawaiian), foreman, in this case a leading man charged with getting out the vote.

WED., FEB. 3 — *Election day. A better result than I hoped for. However our plan of campaign was thorough and well carried out. Fred has done well, and succeeded splendidly. Happy to telephone the news to the Convent.*

FEB. 3. *Fred has done well.* Hayselden, with 1,431 votes, led the Honolulu district.

THURS., FEB. 4 — *The election of all our ticket in Honolulu brings congratulations from all sides. A happy hour at the Br. H.*

Bishop of Olba called on me this evening.

FEB. 4. *The election.* The National or Government party elected eighteen representatives to the 1886 legislature, the Opposition ten. *Pacific Commercial Advertiser*, Feb. 8, 1886.

Bishop of Olba, the Right Reverend Dr. Hermann Koeckemann (Catholic).

FRI., FEB. 5 — *Signed the warrant for the extradition of McCarthy.*

SAT., FEB. 6 — *Mrs Neumann with Miss Eva, Nellie Brown, Miss Gilliland & sister called on me as a surprise party. Bad news from Maui, and so felt a little constrained with my party.*

After they had gone at 6 P.M. I called at the Convent and was comforted with kindly sympathy.

FEB. 6. *Miss Gilliland & sister*, Virginia L. Gilliland (*b.* 1865) and Angela Eva Gilliland (*b.* 1859), daughters of Richard and Rosalie Coffin Gilliland. Probate 278, 291, Archives of Hawaii.

Bad news from Maui. From Maui-Molokai-Lanai the Opposition party won five seats, the Government four. This was the only area where the Government party was defeated.

SUN., FEB. 7 — *Excellent news from Hawaii — more than compensating for the bad from Maui. Numerous congratulations. Sent my cook with a roast duck to the Convent.*

Miss Eva & sister came to congratulate me. Called on Mrs Hendry.

MON., FEB. 8 — *Congratulations of people who want offices.*

At Kakaako — saw Sr Bonaventura — anxiety about S. M.ˢ health.

FEB. 8. *People who want offices.* The Hawaiian word for such people, which was widely used even in the English language newspapers, is *hoopilimeaai* 'hangers-on for food', 'feeders at the trough'.

Sister Bonaventura Caraher, in charge of Malulani branch
hospital at Wailuku, Maui. L. V. Jacks, *Mother Marianne
of Molokai*, p. 44. She arrived at Honolulu with Mother
Marianne and five other sisters on Nov. 8, 1883.

TUES., FEB. 9 — *At Br. H. by 8 A.M. to instruct Mayhew
about removal of two small houses. S. M. and Sr
Bonaventura at my house.*

FEB. 9. *Edward E. Mayhew,* carpenter and contractor.
McKenney's *Hawaiian Directory,* 1888.

WED., FEB. 10 — *Called on Her Majesty in the morning to
remind her of visit to K[apiolani] Home. The Queen
visited the Home at 3 P.M. H. M. much affected by her
visit. She reverences the Sisters and is inclined to be a
Catholic.*

FEB. 10. *Queen's visit to Kapiolani Home* for girls, at Kakaako.
Henri Berger's Royal Hawaiian Band accompanied fifty
inmates singing *The Hawaiian Lepers' Hymn,* of
"peculiarly plaintive character . . . and profoundly pathetic
effect." *Pacific Commercial Advertiser,* Feb. 11, 1886.
   The Kapiolani Home, named after the queen, was dedicated
on Nov. 9, 1885. It was one of Gibson's pet projects. He
spoke at the dedication and also celebrated the second
anniversary of the arrival of the Franciscan sisters.
Dedication of Kapiolani Home (Honolulu, 1885). *The
Hawaiian Lepers' Hymn,* words by King Kalakaua, English
version by Gibson, appears on p. 4 of this pamphlet.

THURS., FEB. 11 — *An excursion to my beach place,*
Kapiolani Park. S. M., Sr Bonaventura, Martha, and Mary
Charles — with the ten girls of Kapiolani Home. An
omnibus & a carriage.
I lunched with them.

FEB. 11. *Sisters Martha and Mary Charles* were in the second
group of Franciscan sisters to arrive from Syracuse, N.Y.
This group came in April 1885, and included also Sisters
Benedicta and Leopoldina. A. Mouritz, *Brief World*
History of Leprosy (Honolulu: privately printed, 1943),
p. 45.

FRI., FEB. 12 — *At Br. H. to superintend moving of small*
house. S. M. recommended to write to M[ary] T[anner]
in London. I did not like it.
At the Queen's garden party this aft.

FEB. 12. *Mary Tanner.* Was Marianne encouraging Gibson
to rekindle an old flame? See also diary entry of Mar. 12,
1886. (See Addresses, 1886 Diary, for Tanner address.)
Gibson met her in Paris in 1854 when he was in Europe
pursuing a claim against the Dutch government for his
imprisonment in the Dutch East Indies.

Queen's garden party, to celebrate the twelfth anniversary
of Kalakaua's accession. Queen Kapiolani received,
assisted by Princesses Liliuokalani and Likelike. The
palace was opened to the public. *Hawaiian Gazette*,
Feb. 16, 1886.

SAT., FEB. 13 — *Wrote to Mr Spreckels. Accompanied Mr*
Putnam, U.S. Consul, to the Convent to take

acknowledgement of S. M. to a power of attorney she sends to Syracuse.

I remained to spend a happy hour. Call of Sir Alexander Steward and Mr Davies.

FEB. 13. *Claus Spreckels* (1828–1908), the sugar king of Hawaii and California, and the financial angel (some would say "devil") of the Hawaiian government. He also had some control over Gibson and Kalakaua by means of personal loans to them. Spreckels appears later in these diaries, mainly in connection with the fight over a loan bill in the legislature.

Marianne's power of attorney to Syracuse. St. Anthony's Convent, Syracuse, N.Y., was the motherhouse of the Third Order of St. Francis.

John H. Putnam, U.S. consul general, Honolulu.

Sir Alexander Steward [Stuart], premier of New South Wales, Australia, 1883–1885. He was on his way to London as one of the commissioners to the Colonial and Indian Exhibition. He died there in June 1886. *Dictionary of National Biography*, vol. 19, 70–71.

Theo. H. Davies, British-born director of the well-known Honolulu sugar and mercantile firm of the same name. He was British vice consul at Honolulu and an old friend of Sir Alexander Stuart. *Daily Bulletin*, Feb. 13, 1886; *Pacific Commercial Advertiser*, Feb. 15, 1886.

SUN., FEB. 14 — *Arrival of* City of Pekin. *I went out on board tug* Eleu, *outside of harbor, to hasten the health clearance. Arrival of R. W. Irwin with Japanese immigrants.*

FEB. 14. *Robert Walker Irwin,* Hawaiian consul general and commissioner of immigration, Tokyo, an American

businessman living in Japan and married to a Japanese. He
brought a convention providing for immigration of contract
labor to Hawaii. It was signed in Tokyo on Jan. 28, 1886, by
Foreign Minister Count Inouye, former business associate
of Irwin. R. S. Kuykendall, *The Hawaiian Kingdom,
1874–1893* (Honolulu: University of Hawaii Press, 1967),
pp. 155, 170–171.

MON., FEB. 15 — *The Jap. Consul Gen¹ Ando called upon
me in company with Mr R. W. Irwin.*

*At Kakaako with S. M. Carpenters putting on new locks
in rooms — and enclosed a small space with wire netting
for new fernery.*

FEB. 15. *Taro Ando,* new consul general and diplomatic agent
for Japan, had arrived with Robert W. Irwin on Feb. 14.
Ando had been consul at Shanghai. He brought to his
new office "the reputation of a gentleman of culture and
education, an excellent English scholar and great experience
in the public service." *Daily Bulletin,* Feb. 15, 1886.

TUES., FEB. 16 — *Unwell yest. aft. — a depression — a
troublesome ailment.*

Dr and Mrs Webb at the house.

WED., FEB. 17 — *Better in health — the depression relieved.
S. M. telephoned to me to come — took my lunch at the
Convent — a happy and inspiring visit.*

*I called on Mr Ando this morning. He called on me with
his wife this evening.*

THURS., FEB. 18 — *Got some white stone for new fernery.*

FRI., FEB. 19 — *Mrs Strong and Mrs Julius Smith took dinner with me.*

    K[akaako] ["At K- in the afternoon" erased]

FEB. 19. *Mrs. Julius Smith*, wife of the superintendent of public works.

SAT., FEB. 20 — *Much disappointed on arrival of* Kinau, *not to see Talula and the children.*

SUN., FEB. 21 — *Mrs Julius Smith called this forenoon.*

MON., FEB. 22 — *At Br. H. this* P.M.

TUES., FEB. 23 — *Return of the King per* W. G. Hall.

FEB. 23. *Return of the King.* There was much ceremony at the wharf because Kalakaua had been away almost a month, mainly at Kailua, Kona, on the island of Hawaii. Gibson was among those greeting him. "The King's Arrival," *Daily Bulletin*, Feb. 24, 1886.

WED., FEB. 24 — *At Br. H. this* P.M. *Have ordered Mayhew to construct a small conservatory, or glass house for plants, to be attached to the Convent of St Francis — a present to the Sisters.*

    The King spent an hour & a half at my house this evening.

23

THURS., FEB. 25 — *The King paid another long visit to my house this evening.*

FRI., FEB. 26 — *The King requests me to make out an appointment for Gresly Jackson as Principal of Reformatory School. I have agreed to do so — but I dislike the importunity of Jackson with the King.*
At Kakaako 4 P.M.

FEB. 26. *George E. Gresly* [*Gresley*] *Jackson*, retired navigating lieutenant of the British navy. His best (or worst) claim to fame was his command of Hawaii's one-ship navy, the *Kaimiloa* (manned largely by reform school boys) on its unfortunate mission to Samoa in May 1887.

SUN., FEB. 28 — *Talula, Fred, the children, Lita* [?] *and Kahaulelio all returned per* Kinau *this morning* — 7½ A.M.
I left a note at Kakaako for S. M. early this morning.

MON., MAR. 1 — *A meeting of Board of Educaⁿ to appoint Jackson — the King's wish. Arrival of the* Stirlingshire.
At Kakaako — M. — much headache.
Rumors of mobs gathering [*not clear: followed by erasures and scrawls*]

TUES., MAR. 2 — *The King proposing large increase of military. I called upon Mr Taro Ando — also upon Mr Dare at Hotel.*
Caught cold. Much wind and rain.

MAR. 2. *John T. Dare*, a California lawyer brought to Honolulu to protect Claus Spreckels' interests. King Kalakaua quickly granted Dare letters of denization, giving him rights of Hawaiian citizenship. On June 30, under pressure from Spreckels, the king appointed Dare attorney general. In October 1886 Dare failed to push through a Spreckels-sponsored amendment to a loan bill. In the resulting break between Spreckels and the king, the cabinet fell.

WED., MAR. 3 — *Introduced Mr Dare to the King at Healani Palace.*

An invalid today.

Sent turkey to Kakaako.

The King distresses me with a Nicaraguan canal scheme.

MAR. 3. *Healani Palace.* The cabinet council minutes for 1886 generally show meetings at Iolani Palace, the royal residence. Occasionally the minutes are headed *Healani Hale.* This may have been a section of the palace or a separate building. Possibly this was the king's waterfront boathouse. The king's canoe club was called the Healani club.

THURS., MAR. 4 — *Mr Neumann took lunch with me. He is anxious about the King's military and opium projects.*

I went to Immigration depot to see crofters engaged by me.

MAR. 4. *King's military and opium projects.* The king loved military ceremony and parades. But he may also have sensed, more clearly than either Neumann or Gibson, the need to arm because of the unrest which culminated in the revolution of 1887.

25

An opium licensing law passed by the legislature of 1886 got the king into trouble, and contributed to the revolution.

Crofters. Eight Scottish crofters, with three dogs, came by the British ship *Stirlingshire.* Five were to go to Gibson's Lanai sheep ranch. *Pacific Commercial Advertiser,* Mar. 5, 6, 1886.

FRI., MAR. 5 — *The King anxious on account of supposed want of harmony among Ministers. Neumann supposed to be changing, without consultation, arrangement to recover money on acct of water works.*

At Br. H. this aft. Came away dissatisfied.

MAR. 5. *Water works.* See diary entry of Jan. 22, 1886, and corresponding note.

SAT., MAR. 6 — *10 A.M.* — *Exchanged ratifications of Immigration Convention with Mr Ando.*

At Br. H. by 11 A.M. hoping for a happier mood — but not so. Kind interest of Sr Leopoldina.

MAR. 6. *Immigration Convention* with Japan was approved by cabinet council on Feb. 25. The king appointed Gibson as commissioner to exchange ratifications. See Cabinet Council Minute Book, Feb. 25, 1886, Archives of Hawaii.

Sister Leopoldina arrived at Honolulu from Syracuse in April 1885 and was placed in charge of the women and girls at Kakaako. She went to Kalaupapa, Molokai (with Mother Marianne and Sister Vincent), in November 1888, and described her years there "as the forty happiest years of

my life." Eileen O'Brien, "Happy Years among the Molokai
Lepers," *Paradise of the Pacific*, August 1946, pp. 12–14, 30.

SUN., MAR. 7 — *Attended grand mass at Cathedral, 10 A.M.
In pew with Madam Feer, the Misses Feer, and young
Mr Feer.*

*Cabinet Council — subject, Proclamation [of] opening
of Assembly.*

MON., MAR. 8 — *The King received Mr Feer Jr presented by
me.*

*At Br. H. — pleasant — yet a much quieter tone —
perhaps Lent.*

TUES., MAR. 9 — *Privy Council — Friday opening of
Assembly.*

*Cabinet Council — allow Gulick to overdraw on acct
of Survey Dept. I was much opposed to this.*

Departure of the King per W. G. Hall.

MAR. 9. *Gulick to overdraw.* The cabinet resolved that
Gulick's drafts for certain salaries in the survey bureau be
charged to an indemnity account. Cabinet Council
Minute Book, Mar. 7, 1886, Archives of Hawaii. Gulick's
management of the interior department was considered
somewhat inept, and was often questioned by Gibson and
others.

Departure of the king, with the Royal Hawaiian Band,
for Hookena, Hawaii, to take part in a Sunday school
convention. *Pacific Commercial Advertiser,* Mar. 9, 1886.

WED., MAR. 10 — *At Br. H. — a pleasant hour.*

THURS., MAR. 11 — *Good sleep last night. An improved
tone of health — yet a certain dainty spirit of melancholia.
Too sentimental for my years.*
   Very busy with reports.

FRI., MAR. 12 — *Letter to Mary Tanner to go per* Mararoa.
*Also sent newspapers. Tender reminiscences of Paris — but
nothing like* ["Kakaako" *erased, then scrawled over*]

MAR. 12. *Reminiscences of Paris.* See diary entry of Feb. 12,
   1886, and accompanying note. In 1854 Gibson had attached
   himself to the U.S. embassy in Paris, to the embarrassment of
   the ambassador who was admonished by the U.S. secretary
   of state.

SAT., MAR. 13 — *Busy with reports. Keep Webb, Wright
and Roche hard at work. Also three translators at work all
the time.*
   *An hour at Kakaako. The Mother wants me to request
Dr Arning to make a professional visit to Sr Rosalia.*

MAR. 13. *Joseph Sykes Webb,* secretary of the department of
   foreign affairs. For a short time in 1884 he had been editor
   of the *Advertiser.* He served as paymaster of the navy
   on the May 1887 mission of the *Kaimiloa* to Samoa.
   (Actually, he served as informer for Gibson.)

   W. J. Roche, a government clerk who was "collecting
   information and arranging statistics for the bureau of
   immigration." C. T. Gulick to C. P. Iaukea, Interior

4444

Department Letter Book 27, Mar. 1, 1886, Archives of
Hawaii.

SUN., MAR. 14 — *Sent for Dr Arning — requested him to
make a professional call on Sister Rosalia.*

MON., MAR. 15 — *Arrival of* Mararoa. *Departure of Mr
R. W. Irwin, Mr Ando and Mr Nakayama.
Trouble with the crofters.
An hour at Kakaako.*

MAR. 15. *Departure of R. W. Irwin, Taro Ando, and G. O.
Nakayama,* on inspection tour among Japanese immigrants
on Maui and Hawaii. *Pacific Commercial Advertiser,* Mar. 16,
1886. G. O. Nakayama (or Nacayama) was special inspector
of Japanese immigrants for the Hawaiian board of
immigration. Not to be confused with Kakichiro Nakayama
who was secretary of the Japanese consulate, Honolulu.

TUES., MAR. 16 — *Mailed letters to A. Hoffnung.
Call of Miss Florence Winter.*

MAR. 16. *Abraham Hoffnung,* Hawaii's chargé d'affaires in
London. He had a great deal to do with preliminary
negotiations for a Hawaiian loan in London, which
became the subject of much acrimony in the 1886
legislature. See R. S. Kuykendall, *The Hawaiian Kingdom,
1874–1893,* p. 294.

Florence Winter, a teacher. The next year she got a
one-year license to teach in the public schools. *Daily
Bulletin,* Sept. 23, 1887.

WED., MAR. 17 — *Sent ducks &c for dinner to Convent at Kakaako. Compliment to Sister Rosalia.*

THURS., MAR. 18 — *Made a few minutes' call at Kakaako about 11 A.M.*

With Talula, Fred, Walter and Lucy at Music Hall — ventriloquism of Millis.

MAR. 18. *Fred W. Millis*, "king of ventriloquists." "A half dozen lifeless figures were made to look, sing, and talk like animated beings. . . . The audience was fairly uproarious with delight." *Daily Bulletin*, Mar. 17, 1886. The *Music Hall*, also known as the Hawaiian Opera House, was next to Gibson's home on King Street off Palace Square.

FRI., MAR. 19 — *At work on Education and Health reports. Vanity of Prof. Scott. Faithful work and modesty of Mr Roche. Disagreement between Wright and Hendry.*

MAR. 19. *Marion M. Scott*, principal of Fort Street School, served in 1885 as acting inspector general of schools. He had spent ten years in Japan where he helped to start a teachers' college. *Men of Hawaii* (1921), p. 353.

Eugene R. Hendry, an employee of the board of health. He had once been deputy collector of customs, and had recently returned from San Francisco where he was employed at the Hawaiian consulate. *Pacific Commercial Advertiser*, Mar. 8, 1886; *Hawaiian Gazette*, Mar. 9, Apr. 6, 1886.

SAT., MAR. 20 — *Busy with Education and Immigration reports. Miss Albro arrived from Lahaina.*

K------ ["A happy hour at Kakaako" erased]

MAR. 20. *Jane Albro*, public school teacher on the island of Lanai. *Pacific Commercial Advertiser*, Aug. 15, 1887.

K., abbreviation often used to mean "at Kakaako" or "visit to Kakaako."

SUN., MAR. 21 — *With the King this morning. H. M. distrusts H. A. P. Carter. Will advance Iaukea as our representative Hawaiian diplomat.*

MAR. 21. *Henry A. P. Carter* (1835–1891), Hawaii's minister to the United States, 1883–1891. He was a prominent businessman and held many positions in Hawaii's government. He was instrumental in negotiating the U.S.-Hawaii reciprocity treaty of 1876. Gibson's statement about the king distrusting him may reflect Gibson's own dislike of Carter as one of the "Fort Street Church people." Kuykendall calls Carter "probably the ablest diplomat ever to serve the Hawaiian kingdom." R. S. Kuykendall, *The Hawaiian Kingdom, 1874–1893*, p. 491.

Curtis P. Iaukea (1855–1940), collector general of customs. On Aug. 30, 1886, he was appointed royal chamberlain, and on Oct. 4 he became governor of Oahu. In April 1887 as ambassador to Great Britain, he accompanied Queen Kapiolani to Queen Victoria's Jubilee. He had a truly astonishing career of public service from 1878 to his death, and must be ranked as a great Hawaiian statesman. For sketch of his career, see *Hawaiian Church Chronicle* (Honolulu), April 1940.

TUES., MAR. 23 — *Went with Dower to Kakaako to arrange for steam baths for lepers. Afterwards a pleasant half hour.*

Bought lands at auction — Maunalei $4650 — Pakala $1650 — Queen St lots $5710.

MAR. 23. *J. A. Dower*, ship's carpenter and boatbuilder, fitted up a boiler at Kakaako that would heat 140 gallons of water in five minutes by a jet of steam. *Daily Bulletin*, Apr. 3, 1886. The steam baths were part of the Dr. Goto treatment for leprosy.

Lands at auction. These were among the lands of Queen Emma's estate: Maunalei, about 3,400 acres on Lanai; Pakala, slightly more than an acre at Lahaina, Maui; Queen Street lots, about an acre in Honolulu. *Pacific Commercial Advertiser*, Mar. 24, 1886.

WED., MAR. 24 — *Much annoyed to learn that Gulick had spent on Dept accts proceeds of Portuguese immigration.*

Protest of immigration drafts $40,000 — Spreckels would not help.

An hour at Kakaako.

MAR. 24. *Spreckels would not help.* This was part of Spreckels' campaign to block a Hawaiian loan in London. He did not want any poaching on his preserve as the chief creditor of the Hawaiian government.

THURS., MAR. 25 — *Resolve to protect immigration drafts. Spreckels wants our credit with Hoffnung in London to be injured. Wants to prevent chances of an English loan.*

["Paid the drafts" erased and crossed over] About all our treasury balance gone.

A half hour at Kakaako.

FRI., MAR. 26 — *Interview with S. M. Damon. Surprise[d] to know that we do not owe Mr Spreckels a dollar on special loan acct. Bishop & Co will not call for $20,000 bonds. I ordered payment of Hoffnung immigration drafts. The King wants to send the Queen abroad. Examination.*

MAR. 26. *Samuel Mills Damon,* partner in Bishop & Co. bank, was a member of the privy council, 1884. He served the Kingdom, the Provisional Government, the Republic, and the Territory of Hawaii as minister of finance. *Men of Hawaii* (1917), p. 81.

Hoffnung immigration drafts. In London, Hoffnung helped officially with Portuguese immigration to Hawaii. He also had a business interest in such immigration.

SAT., MAR. 27 — *Bonds provided for — drafts paid — two great dangers tided over — yet an empty treasury — and the King wants so much.*

Annoyed by Trousseau, Arning & Neumann. A happy hour at Kakaako. Pleasure of my ears [?]. Miss Albro comes to visit us. The King, Kapena & family here.

MAR. 27. *Dr. George Trousseau* (1833–1894) came to Honolulu in 1872, served as physician and chamberlain to King Lunalilo. In 1873, on Trousseau's advice, a strong effort was made to segregate lepers. He examined many

persons at a newly established Kalihi leper detention
station. He had many run-ins with Gibson on board of
health policies. Biographical sketch in F. J. Halford, *Nine
Doctors and God* (Honolulu: University of Hawaii Press,
1954), pp. 303–304.

SUN., MAR. 28 — *A sleepless night. Indoors all day with
cough.*

MON., MAR. 29 — *The King wants $6800 for his guard this
month. Only let him have $1700.*

MAR. 29. *The King's Guards* (regular troops) and six volunteer
military companies, including the Honolulu Rifles,
constituted the military forces of the kingdom. R. S.
Kuykendall, *The Hawaiian Kingdom, 1874—1893*, p. 352.
The appropriation for the Guards for the two years
ending Mar. 31, 1886, was $88,000.

TUES., MAR. 30 — *Made an arrangement with Mr
Sprecke[l]s for $50,000. Deposit Spreckels & Co
certificates & use special deposit funds.*

A few minutes at Br. H. to start Dower on steam boiler.

*The King left per W. G. Hall. Blank commission for
Kaulukou.*

MAR. 30. *Per W. G. Hall*, should be per *Kinau*. The king
was going to the island of Hawaii. *Pacific Commercial
Advertiser*, Mar. 31, 1886.

Blank commission, possibly as postmaster general, a position to
which John Lot Kaulukou was appointed Apr. 15.

WED., MAR. 31 — *$30,000 deposited in the treasury.*

An hour at Kakaako.

Pay day is satisfactorily met. Sent 2 doz Ginger Ale to Sisters.

THURS., APRIL 1 — *Got deed for lands purchased.*

A few minutes at Br. H.

R. W. Irwin wants to have his advances for doctors & interpreters allowed — not authorized.

Fred arranging For. Office accts.

FRI., APRIL 2 — *Agree with Gulick to allow Irwin's advances — $5800.*

A few minutes at Br. H.

Sent swing for girls at K. Home.

SAT., APRIL 3 — *At Br. H. this afternoon.*

SUN., APRIL 4 — *Attended mass at the Catholic Cathedral 10 A.M.*

MON., APRIL 5 — *Busy revising Wright's work on leprosy report.*

At Br. H.

WED., APRIL 7 — *Dada (Fred) shows symptoms of fever — a low malarial fever.*

At Br. H. with S. M.

APR. 7. "Dada," *Frederick Howard Hayselden* (1879–1955), son of Talula and Frederick Harrison Hayselden. The somewhat delicate child survived to devote most of his adult life to heavy construction work, including road-building. During World War II he served in the U.S. Army Corps of Engineers. Obituary, *Honolulu Advertiser*, Mar. 16, 1955; *Honolulu Star-Bulletin*, Mar. 16, 1955.

THURS., APRIL 8 — *Dada continues feverish. Dr Trousseau's letter — will not attend on acct of my alledged* [sic] *attacks upon him. Fred called on the Dr & satisfied him of the absurdity of his suspicions. Sr Rosalia called with report.*

With Fred at Mr Ando's party this ev.

APR. 8. *Ando's party*, at the Japanese consulate. "The driveway and house were illuminated . . . with a profusion of Japanese lanterns; the interior of the house was tastefully decorated with evergreens, flowers, etc.; . . . After an hour or two of social chat, refreshments were bountifully served." Princess Liliuokalani and Princess Likelike and practically the entire Honolulu consular corps were there. *Daily Bulletin*, Apr. 9, 1886.

FRI., APRIL 9 — *Departure of* Zealandia. *Adieux to R. W. Irwin, Eva Neumann, Mr Collins & others.*

An hour at Br. H.

APR. 9. *Departure of Zealandia*, more festive than usual because this was the first sailing under the Hawaiian flag. The ceremony was marred only by the absence of the Royal Hawaiian Band, which had not yet returned with the king from Hawaii. The fact of Hawaiian registry of the *Zealandia* was credited to Claus Spreckels. *Daily Bulletin*, Apr. 9, 1886; *Pacific Commercial Advertiser*, Apr. 10, 1886.

G. *Collins* and wife, not otherwise identified, passengers on *Zealandia. Pacific Commercial Advertiser*, Apr. 10, 1886.

SAT., APRIL 10 — *Sent my carriage at 10* A.M. *to give Sisters a drive. Sr Marᵉ & Sr Rosalia drove by the house — a few minutes call.*

Dada remains feverish.

SUN., APRIL 11 — *Wea. — warm & windy — The King returned at 6.30* A.M. *per* Kinau. *Had a long interview with H. M. — at Palace from 10 to 11.30* A.M. *Heart heavy and weary — although all is promising in business & politics.*

MON., APRIL 12 — *Spent an hour this* A.M. *with the King. H. M. pleased with news from For. Off. London — Lord Roseberry's letter to Sir Sackville West.*

An hour at Kakaako.

APR. 12. *Lord Roseberry* [Rosebery] (British foreign minister) *to Sir Sackville West* (British minister to U.S.). May refer to letter of Feb. 18, 1886: "I have to request you to inform Mr. Carter [Hawaiian minister to the United States] that H. M.'s Govt would not be opposed to a scheme whereby the independence of these Islands [not yet occupied by the great powers] should be secured by a self denying agreement among the Powers in order to afford their inhabitants the opportunity of forming settled goverts with the assistance and advice of Hawaii." British Public Records Office, FO 115/775. The king and Gibson doubtless saw this as a green light for Hawaii's proposed expansionist policy in the Pacific.

TUES., APRIL 13 — *Department work crowding on our hands.*
Little Dada improving, but much reduced in flesh.

WED., APRIL 14 — *An hour at Kakaako.*
Dada remains languid and without appetite.

THURS., APRIL 15 — *S. M. quite unwell.*

FRI., APRIL 16 — *Cannot induce Dada to eat — very thin.*

SUN., APRIL 18 — *The great fire — was with the King in the midst of it.*
Death of Mrs Kapena.

APR. 18. *The great fire,* wiped out about sixty acres of the
Chinese section of the city, did damage estimated at $1.5
million, and left several thousand persons homeless. *Pacific
Commercial Advertiser*, Apr. 19, 1886; *Daily Bulletin*,
Apr. 19, 1886.
   King Kalakaua was said to be a fire buff. "He did
excellent work urging on the willing men and exerting
himself to the utmost to stay . . . the raging flames. Again
and again did the men under his command strive to stay
the flames, and again and again were they driven back."
Hawaiian Gazette, Apr. 20, 1886.

Death of Mrs. John M. Kapena, from a heart condition
apparently aggravated by the excitement of the fire. She
was the daughter of the Hawaiian historian, David Malo.
Hawaiian Gazette, Apr. 20, 1886.

MON., APRIL 19 — *A Cabinet meeting, and Privy Council —*
$10,000 for the sufferers by fire.
A call at Kakaako — took [erased]

TUES., APRIL 20 — *Got some flowers in pots and took to Convent.*

   Funeral of Mrs Kapena.

   Neumann sick — an attack of pleurisy.

WED., APRIL 21 — *Annoyed to see a proclamation by Gulick issued without consulting me. Saw the King. A Cabinet meeting at Neuman[n]'s house, he being sick. Result — a Cabinet Committee of which I am chairman, to carry out measures for restoration of city.*

APR. 21. *Proclamation by Gulick*, essentially to the effect that repairs to wooden buildings must not be made, that repairs or restoration must be with fireproof materials, and that sanitary requirements would be strictly enforced. Considering that thousands of people were homeless, it seems a brusque, insensitive proclamation. Text in *Pacific Commercial Advertiser*, Apr. 21, 1886.

Cabinet Committee. Gulick was the other member. Frank H. Austin was appointed agent for the committee. *Pacific Commercial Advertiser*, Apr. 20, 1886.

THURS., APRIL 22 — *Capt Blackburne of* Heroine *and Mr Wodehouse called on me.*

   A happy hour at Kakaako.

   The Queen will not go abroad.

   Miss Cotta Mist called.

APR. 22. *H.B.M.S. Heroine, Capt. F. R. Blackburne*, arrived Honolulu Apr. 16 from Coquimbo, Chile, enroute to Hong Kong. *Pacific Commercial Advertiser*, Apr. 17, 1886.

The Queen will not go abroad. She went the next year, in April, to attend Queen Victoria's Jubilee.

Miss Cotta Mist, teacher at the Royal School. *Pacific Commercial Advertiser,* July 24, 1886.

─────────────────────────────────

FRI., APRIL 23 — *The King told me as a piece of good news that the Queen had decided not to go abroad. I am glad on acct of not having to find the money for trav⁹ expenses.*

SAT., APRIL 24 — *Two Sisters, Benedicta and Ludovica, arrived from Wailuku.*
Bad cough last night.
Arrival of Mararoa.

─────────────────────────────────

APR. 24. *Sister Benedicta* (*d.* July 26, 1942) arrived from Syracuse in April 1885. (St. Anthony's Convent there was the motherhouse of the Third Order of St. Francis.) She was sent to Malulani Hospital, Wailuku, Maui, where she served until 1888, and then returned to the Kapiolani Home. In 1916 she became superior of Molokai, relieving Mother Marianne who was in failing health. A. Mouritz, *Brief World History of Leprosy,* pp. 46–47.

Sister Ludovica was one of the original group of Franciscan sisters who had arrived with Mother Marianne on Nov. 8, 1883.

─────────────────────────────────

SUN., APRIL 25 — *Attended high mass at Cathedral. At Kakaako 1* P.M. *— took lunch there. Met Sisters Benedicta and Ludovica. With S. M. — remained till 5* P.M.

MON., APRIL 26 — *Reception of Capt Blackburne 10* A.M. *at Palace.*

Cabinet Council 11 A.M. — Finance Report — King's Speech.

APR. 26. *Cabinet Council* approved draft of the king's speech
for the opening of the legislature. Cabinet Council Minute
Book, Archives of Hawaii, Apr. 26, 1886. Beyond question
the speech was mainly Gibson's work.

TUES., APRIL 27 — *At Kakaako.*

THURS., APRIL 29 — *At Kakaako.*
    Busy revising Board of Health report.

FRI., APRIL 30 — *Opening of the Legislative Assembly. Mrs
Gulick and Mrs Neumann the only ladies present
connected with the Govt. The Judges' wives and others
staid away, as a mark of disfavor to the ministry.*

APR. 30. *Opening of the Legislative Assembly.* The pomp and
pageantry — royal procession, troops in full dress, the
band, flowers, kahili bearers, booming of cannon — are
fully described in the newspapers. The description of what
Mesdames Neumann and Gulick wore emphasized their
presence (Gibson's statement that they were "the only
ladies present connected with the government" was an
exaggeration. There were other wives, though of lesser
rank, present.) Mrs. Neumann: "a dress of Japanese
embroidered crepe and white satin, with Duchesse lace
trimmings and feather tips." Mrs. Gulick: "a dress of fawn
colored moire antique, with Brussels point lace and pink
feather trimmings." Both women wore diamonds. *Pacific
Commercial Advertiser*, May 1, 1886.

❧§1886§❧

SAT., MAY 1 — *At Kakaako.*
At work on For. Office report.

SUN., MAY 2 — *Mr Spreckels at the house. He suggests a loan of $2,000,000 — $1,000,000 to take up all outstanding bonds & the other million for immigration & inter[nal] improvements.*

MON., MAY 3 — *Admiral Seymour of the* Triumph *and Mr Seymour call upon me.*
At Kakaako. Departure of Sister Benedicta per Likelike. *I escorted her on board.*

MAY 3. *Rear Admiral Sir Michael Culme Seymour*, baronet (1836–1920), commander of the Pacific Squadron, 1885–1887. The *Triumph* was his flagship. *Pacific Commercial Advertiser*, May 1, 1886. *Who Was Who, 1916–1928* (London, 1967).

TUES., MAY 4 — *Reception of Admiral Seymour at Palace. I attended in full uniform.*

WED., MAY 5 — *Quiet spirit in the Legislature — no opposition so far.*
A happy hour at Kakaako.
Procured ticket for Mrs Dr Webb to go to & return from San Francisco, for which I paid $150.

MAY 5. *Mrs. Dr. Webb* has a Germanic flavor. "Mrs. Dr.," not now standard English, is precisely equivalent to German *Frau Doktor*.

THURS., MAY 6 — *Ball at Palace in honor of Admiral Seymour. I went. Talula & Fred staid at home on acct of death of his mother. I escorted Mrs Gulick. Promenade with Mrs Neumann, Mrs Ando, Fanny. The judges' wives at the ball.*

MAY 6. *Palace ball for Adm. Seymour.* "The Palace was illuminated with many colored lights, and the grounds were lit up with torches. . . . Dancing was kept up with great spirit. . . . The uniforms of the naval officers and the gay dresses of the many young ladies set off by the more sombre but perhaps more artistic dresses of the elder ladies made a very pretty and animated scene. . . . As midnight struck and cloaks and shawls were called for there was a universal verdict from many a rose bud mouth of a 'thorough success.' " *Hawaiian Gazette*, May 11, 1886.

Death of Fred's mother, Mrs. Thomas Hayselden, at Los Gatos, California. *Pacific Commercial Advertiser*, Apr. 26, 1886.

Fanny, Mrs. Richard F. Bickerton.

FRI., MAY 7 — *Departure of* Zealandia — *Mrs E. C. Webb leaves.*

SAT., MAY 8 — *Presented For. Off. Report to the Assembly. Took lot of ferns to the Convent — a pleasant time with the Sisters. Rosalia & Charles better. Mr Spreckels requested me to arrange for an audience at Palace — Sir Anthony Musgrave and others.*

MAY 8. *Sir Anthony Musgrave* (1828–1888), governor of
Queensland, Australia, 1883–1888. *Modern English
Biography*, ed. Frederic Boase, p. 1058.

SUN., MAY 9 — *Presented Sir Anthony and Lady Musgrave,
Charles Service Esq and Mrs Service, Genl Freemantle
and Mr Prichard to the King at Iolani Palace, in company
with Mr Spreckels.*

MAY 9. *Charles Service.* Current newspapers and the Iolani
Palace Visitors Book for this date show only James
Service (1823–1899), premier of Victoria, Australia,
1883–1885.

General Sir Arthur J. L. Freemantle [Fremantle] (1835–1901),
governor of Suakim, 1884–1885; governor of Malta,
1894–1899. *Who Was Who, 1897–1915* (London, 1920).

Herbert C. Prichard, aide-de-camp to Sir Anthony Musgrave.
All these people were merely passing visitors.

MON., MAY 10 — *At Kakaako — 11 A.M.*
[*one word erased*]

TUES., MAY 11 — *On board* Triumph *at 10 A.M. Cordially
received by Admiral Seymour. J. Webb with me —
15 guns.*

WED., MAY 12 — *Worry in the House about Copyist &c.
At Kakaako — no* [*a word scrawled out*]

THURS., MAY 13 — *A moderate day in the House. Lunch at
the Palace. Birthday of Prince Keliiahonui.*

MAY 13. *Birthday of Prince Edward Abel Keliiahonui,* his seventeenth. Princess Poomaikelani gave a birthday luau for him at the Palace. She was his aunt, as was Queen Kapiolani. The prince himself, son of Princess Kekaulike (*d.* 1884), was away at school in San Mateo, Calif. He would celebrate only one more birthday (*d.* Sept. 1887). At the luau, Gibson offered toasts to the king and queen. *Pacific Commercial Advertiser,* May 14, 1886.

FRI., MAY 14 — *Some Govt. members voting with Opp. on certain small matters. Makes Gulick and Neumann say native members not to be depended on. I understand otherwise — a mere show of a little opp" to satisfy constituencies. Will be with us in essentials.*

SAT., MAY 15 — *Passed a bad night — a coughing fit — up till 2 A.M. Got 3 hours sleep.*
News from Washington in the House.
Comforted at Kakaako.

MAY 15. *News from Washington.* The *San Francisco Chronicle* of May 5 had reported that the U.S.-Hawaii reciprocity treaty was being renewed with an amendment granting the United States the use of Pearl Harbor, to which native Hawaiians had long been opposed. Gibson had also opposed this amendment. In the legislature he branded the report as false, and so it was — at the time. But when the treaty was finally renewed in 1887, Hawaii had to accept the Pearl Harbor amendment. See R. S. Kuykendall, *The Hawaiian Kingdom, 1874–1893,* pp. 387–397; *Daily Bulletin,* May 15, 1886; *Pacific Commercial Advertiser,* May 17, 1886.

MON., MAY 17 — *An hour at the Convent this morning.*
Curious poem about Marianne sent by Gaunder.

MAY 17. *Joseph E. Gaunder*, hairdresser or barber in Syracuse, N.Y., 1870–1884; insurance and real estate salesman, 1885–1892. His insurance office was at 5 S. Salina St., Syracuse. R. N. Wright, Pres., Onondaga Historical Assn., Syracuse, to Jacob Adler, Sept. 13, 1969.

TUES., MAY 18 — [*"An hour at the Convent this morning" erased*]

WED., MAY 19 — *Half an hour at the Convent this morning. Letter to Miss Tanner per "Wm. G. Irwin."*

THURS., MAY 20 — *Half an hour at the Convent this morning. Sent carriage for S. M. and Sister [?] — an excursion to Manoa.*

　　Letter to Joseph E. Gaunder.

MAY 20. *Manoa*. A lush, green valley, north of Waikiki.

FRI., MAY 21 — *An hour at the Convent this morning. Mrs Altman's importunity to be employed as a teacher.*

MAY 21. *Mrs. A. Altman*, a dressmaker. McKenney's *Hawaiian Directory*, 1884.

SAT., MAY 22 — *At Palace — Reception of S[enho]r Canavarro.*

　　One hour at Convent this morning. With visiting

Committee, at Prison, and Branch Hospital this P.M.

MAY 22. *Reception of Senhor Canavarro.* He was officially
reporting the death of King Ferdinand II of Portugal, and
the accession of King Luiz II.

SUN., MAY 23 — *Ministers with H. M. at Palace. Conference
about economic administration.*

Note per Haiku [?] to S. M. Comforting reply.

*This ev. with the King. Said he wants me 5 years more,
and then would let me go.*

MAY 23. *Haiku,* apparently the name of the messenger. Or
does it mean the message was sent in the form of a Japanese
poem?

The King wants me five years more. Under the head of
"Threatened Men Live Long," the *Pacific Commercial
Advertiser* of May 21 noted the beginning of Gibson's fifth
year as prime minister "with every prospect ... of a long
and prosperous Ministerial career." But during this year
the walls would crumble, and in the next the roof would
fall in.

MON., MAY 24 — *Buoyancy of heart — Joy to call at the
Convent. Ceremonial at the Cathedral. Profession of a nun,
Sacred Hearts. S. M. there. Met her and Sisters Rosalia and
Ludovica afterwards. My joy to meet them in the street.*

MAY 24. *Profession of a nun.* Sister Charlotte became a member
of the Order of the Sacred Hearts. The ceremony, directed by

47

Bishop Hermann, was said to be the first of its kind in
Hawaii. *Pacific Commercial Advertiser*, May 25, 1886;
Hawaiian Gazette, May 25, 1886.

TUES., MAY 25 — *So happy to call at the Convent and see the
dear Sisters.*

Gaunder's newspapers.

THURS., MAY 27 — *A few minutes at the Convent this
morning — again this afternoon. My buoyant heart of the
past days set down a little — questionings & worry of
mind. The King suggests F. H. Austin as a suitable Min.
of Finance. This adds to my depression.*

Gaunder's photo.

MAY 27. *Frank H. Austin,* sugar planter and businessman of
Hilo, Hawaii.

FRI., MAY 28 — *No sleep last night. Depression of spirits.
No Assembly this aft. — I sat in doors all the aft. — quite
alone. Talula and children gone to the Park.*

*The hope at Kakaako is down. Sad news from Dr Brodie
about Dr Hoffman [n] — he has leprosy.*

MAY 28. *Dr. John Brodie,* port physician of board of health,
reports *Dr. Edward Hoffmann has leprosy.* Dr. Hoffmann
(1813–1888) had come to Hawaii from Germany in 1847.
Among other positions, he had served as physician at the
Kalihi leper detention station. He was a fine pianist and

for more than a quarter of a century a leader in Honolulu
society. Biographical sketch in F. J. Halford, *Nine Doctors
and God*, p. 304. This sketch and others do not mention
that he was a leper.

SAT., MAY 29 — *Attack of Thurston in the Assembly. It
will turn to my advantage.*

At Kakaako this P.M. *— restored as usual to my good
spirits whilst there — but when I am away a worry of
mind sets in.*

SUN., MAY 30 — *Talk with the King up stairs at Iolani
[Palace]. ["H. M. wants to" three or four words erased]
Knows of serious charges against him. Wants me to send
him away on some mission.*

*H. M. proposes to visit Kakaako. Paid a visit to Dr
Hoffman[n] — a leper.*

MAY 30. *Serious charges*, probably means *against* Lorrin A.
Thurston, the most vocal and effective member of the
Opposition. The government kept looking in vain for a
way to shut him up.
   Thurston had brought in a resolution to investigate alleged
election frauds by Gibson on the island of Lanai. Thurston
also accused John M. Kapena, minister of finance, of being
drunk on the floor of the House. Then in an "apology" he
aggravated the original charges. *Daily Bulletin*, May 29,
1886; *Pacific Commercial Advertiser*, May 31, June 2, 1886.

MON., MAY 31 — *At the Br. H. 9* A.M. *— a happy hour with
S. M.*

Bitter spirit of the opposition in the House.

On board Australia *this ev. Mr Spreckels warm towards me.*

MAY 31. *On board Australia.* Lavish reception and supper at which the king, almost the entire legislature, and many prominent citizens were present. One purpose was doubtless to lay the groundwork for the Hawaiian subsidy to the Oceanic (Spreckels') steamship line. See two-column account in *Pacific Commercial Advertiser*, June 1, 1886.

TUES., JUNE 1 — *An hour with S. M. this morning. Her care of my personal appearance. The King at Kakaako. Gave to the King Statutes of "Star of Oceania."*

The King with many members at my house this ev. Thurston must be suspended.

JUNE 1. *Star of Oceania.* This royal order, officially created Dec. 16, 1886, had to do with the Kalakaua-Gibson vision of "Hawaiian Primacy of the Pacific." Gordon Medcalf, *Hawaiian Royal Orders* (Honolulu: Oceania Coin Co., 1962), pp. 43–46. *Hawaii Government Gazette*, Feb. 7, 1887.

Thurston must be suspended. In his "apology" on the floor of the legislature, Thurston said: "I have charged in public print over my own signature that the Minister of Finance [J. M. Kapena] was in an intoxicated condition on the floor of the House.... I hereby specifically repeat that charge." A three-hour wrangle followed. Next day Thurston apologized briefly. *Hawaiian Legislature, 1886* (Honolulu: Hawaiian Gazette, 1886), pp. 65–68.

During the argument in the House on June 1, Gibson said that Kapena was a gentleman who had been weighed down by sorrow (the death of his wife) and suffered from ill health. "Who shall charge upon him anything defamatory?" He said Thurston's remarks were appropriate only in the lobby and in the streets. *Pacific Commercial Advertiser*, June 2, 1886.

WED., JUNE 2 — *Thurston's apology — a bitter, unscrupulous man.*

THURS., JUNE 3 — *An hour at Kakaako.*

SAT., JUNE 5 — *A happy hour at Kakaako. The kindly sweet courteous ways of all the Sisters.*

SUN., JUNE 6 — *Attended mass at the Cathedral. Dr Trousseau applied chrysophanic acid to a salt rheum sore.*

MON., JUNE 7 — *Unwell — headache.*
Manoeuvres of Thurston and Kalua. K– was going to slip off per Kinau *to take a run over to Lanai. Fred at the Steamer — to go also. Kalua backed out. Sister Ludovica left per* Likelike.

JUNE 7. *Manoeuvres of Thurston and Kalua*, doubtless related to alleged Lanai election frauds. John W. Kalua (of the Opposition party, as was Thurston) was a representative from Lahaina, Maui.

TUES., JUNE 8 — *At Kakaako. Met Sister Rosalia.*

WED., JUNE 9 — *Confidential letter of H. A. P. Carter about concession of "use" of Pearl Harbor to U.S. Sent to his bro. in law — Frank Judd. Seen by the King. H. M. indignant. I have copy. Dinner at Nacayama's.*

JUNE 9. *Frank Judd*, Albert Francis Judd (1838–1900), chief justice of the supreme court of Hawaii, 1881–1900. Carter was married to Judd's sister, Sybil Augusta, "Gussie." *Judd Family in Hawaii* (Honolulu: Hawaiian Historical Society Genealogical Series No. 3, 1922), pp. 4, 6.

Dinner at Nacayama's. Probably G. O. Nacayama, inspector of Japanese immigration, but possibly K. Nakayama, consulate secretary. Gibson's social and business dealings with the consulate would normally have been through Taro Ando, consul general.

THURS., JUNE 10 — *An hour at Kakaako — a perfect cherry. Proposition to place Father Damien at Kakaako. I am opposed. Ordered the arrest of Pilipo, as a suspected leper.*

JUNE 10. *Father Damien.* Thirteen years earlier Gibson had written of him: "We want to speak of the man . . . who is the first to volunteer to go without purse or scrip, or hope of reward in this life, to minister unto the poor, outcast, hopeless lepers on Molokai. This is the very spirit of Christ." *Nuhou,* May 16, 1873.

Father Damien, Joseph de Veuster (1840–1889), a native of Belgium, entered the Congregation of the Sacred Hearts. In 1864 he went as a missionary to the Hawaiian Islands. After nine years of apostolic work on the island of Hawaii, he went to work at Molokai. He died of leprosy at age 49. In 1969 a statue of him was dedicated in Statuary Hall, Washington, D.C.

Pilipo, a suspected leper. A William Pilipo, age twenty-nine, residence Honolulu, was received at the Molokai settlement Oct. 11, 1887, and died Jan. 18, 1888. Lepers Received at the Settlement, Molokai, Archives of Hawaii.

FRI., JUNE 11 — *Kamehameha Day. At races. Impertinence of Judd at Jockey Club House. Left race course at noon. Lunch at Convent. Happy yet got restless & left early. An unsatisfied and painful yearning — "A lonely old man."*

JUNE 11. *Kamehameha Day [horse] races*, at Kapiolani Park, were a tradition of the day honoring Kamehameha I.

Impertinence of Judd. Probably Charles Hastings Judd, the king's chamberlain.

SAT., JUNE 12 — *An hour at Kakaako. Called away by Lanai Committee. Threats and devilish spirit of Solomona, the Lanai judge.*

Called on Bishop Hermann about Father Damien. Will provide for him at Kalawao.

Uneasy about Mr Spreckels. Apparently some misunderstanding.

JUNE 12. *Solomona Kahoohalahala*, district judge, Lanai.

Will provide for Damien at Kalawao, that is, on Molokai rather than at Kakaako on Oahu.

SUN., JUNE 13 — *Called on Mr Spreckels. All right — had been unusually busy.*

Happy to get a message by telephone from S. M.

MON., JUNE 14 — *Mr Spreckels informed that Neumann had been proposing to the King a message to the House on retrenchment. Saw H.M. — he had not intended to take any action without consulting me.*

TUES., JUNE 15 — *Tedious debate about J. A. Kaukau case. The band at Aholo's place. Meeting at the Palace. The*

King and Mr Spreckels will meet me at my house in the morning.

JUNE 15. *J. A. Kaukau case.* He was a (Government party) representative from Kaanapali, Maui. Thurston tried in vain to unseat him by moving for adoption of a minority report on election irregularities. Attorney General Neumann said Thurston's tactics reminded him of the advice an old lawyer gave his son: "If the facts are against you, stick to the law. If the law is against you, stick to the facts. If *both* are against you, abuse the other side." *Hawaiian Legislature, 1886,* p. 90.

Luther Aholo of Government party, representative from Lahaina, Maui, and vice president of the legislature. He served as minister of interior, Oct. 13, 1886, to June 28, 1887. He was considered one of the ablest of the Hawaiian legislators and was a man of exceptional dignity and presence. Obituaries, *Daily Bulletin,* Mar. 16, 1888; *Pacific Commercial Advertiser,* Mar. 17, 1888; *Hawaiian Gazette,* Mar. 20, 1888.

WED., JUNE 16 — *At Br. H. — about 10 minutes. The King and Mr Spreckels at house at noon. I detained at Assembly — Kaukau case. At Br. H. again this aft. — happy.*

SAT., JUNE 19 — *At Br. H. this afternoon.*

SUN., JUNE 20 — *At high mass. Mad. Feer & daughters. Sent for by Mother Judith.*

JUNE 20. *Mother Judith* (1834–1909), mother superior of the Sacred Hearts Convent on Fort Street and in charge of the boarding and day school there. Born in France and named Marie Brassier, she came to Honolulu in 1859 with the first missionary sisters. Letter, Sister Mary Rose, SS. CC., Honolulu, to Jacob Adler, Aug. 31, 1970.

MON., JUNE 21 — *At Kakaako this morning.*

Cabinet meeting at my house. Mr Spreckels there part of time — but not as taking part in council deliberations.

Message of the King to the Assembly. I dictated part of it — "Prudential considerations of State" &c.

JUNE 21. *Spreckels at cabinet meeting.* He was the main person behind the king's economy message, although Gibson helped draft it. In remarks during the party on the *Australia* on May 31, Spreckels had been outspoken on the need for economy. See editorial, "Practise Economy," *Daily Bulletin*, June 17, 1886.

King's message. Gibson made a long speech in the legislature in support of the message. Thurston said that with the message the king had given the cabinet a well-deserved slap in the face. Gibson said the ministers had given themselves a slap in the face, implying that the message had originated with them. *Daily Bulletin*, June 22, 1886.

TUES., JUNE 22 — *Cabinet meeting continued at Palace. Gulick objects to selling Govt property. He now antagonizes with me — Neumann tries to harmonize.*

JUNE 22. *Selling government property*, i.e., to pay debts without borrowing. See Cabinet Council Minute Book, June 21, 27, 1886.

WED., JUNE 23 — *We approach a Ministerial crisis. Gulick is restive. He does not like my advisory interference. His injudicious enterprises and expenditures involve the Govt.*

THURS., JUNE 24 — *Mr Spreckels at my house. His earnest assurances — but he does not always keep his word. But I doubt not his friendly feeling to me.*

A happy hour at Kakaako.

The King said this ev. that ministry should resign at close of session. Wants to retire Gulick & Neumann — Aholo & Dare for Supreme Court.

SAT., JUNE 26 — *An hour at Kakaako.*

The King tells Spreckels that he will dismiss the ministry and have a new cabinet — Creighton, For. Aff. — Iaukea, Interior — Kanoa, Finance — Dare, Atty. Gen.

JUNE 26. *Robert J. Creighton* (1835–1893), worked as a journalist in Australia, New Zealand, and California, and for ten years was a member of the New Zealand legislature. He came to Honolulu in 1885, presumably at the behest of Spreckels, to take charge of the *Advertiser.* He served as minister of foreign affairs from June 30, 1886, to Oct. 13, 1886. In June 1887, he gave up editorship of the *Advertiser,* when it became a semiofficial government organ. *Daily Bulletin,* June 1, 1886; R. S. Kuykendall, *The Hawaiian Kingdom, 1874–1893,* pp. 275, 281, 292, and 346.

Paul P. Kanoa, governor of Kauai, 1881–1886; member of house of nobles, 1882–1892; member of privy council, 1883–1888; minister of finance, June 30, 1886, to June 28, 1887. Obituary, *Pacific Commercial Advertiser,* Mar. 19, 1895.

SUN., JUNE 27 — *Cabinet meeting — my proposition to sell public property in order to meet our obligations. Not acquiesced in by Gulick.*

MON., JUNE 28 — *Mr Spreckels showed me a note from the King proposing Iaukea, For. Aff. — Hassinger, Int. — Kanoa, Finance — Aholo, Atty. Gen. Spreckels indignant — sent an angry note to H. M. by hands of Sam Parker.*

I saw the King this ev. — will let me make a new ministry.

JUNE 28. *John Adair Hassinger*, chief clerk of interior department. He liked to play soldier, which may have endeared him to the ceremony-loving king. Hassinger was captain of a juvenile military company that wore fancy uniforms and drilled with real rifles. *Pacific Commercial Advertiser*, June 25, 1886; *Daily Bulletin*, June 24, 1886.

Sam Parker, major and equerry-in-waiting to the king. He was a member of the house of nobles, 1886–1890, and foreign minister in the cabinet of Queen Liliuokalani at the time of her overthrow in January 1893. Obituary, *Honolulu Star-Bulletin*, Mar. 20, 1920; *Pacific Commercial Advertiser*, Mar. 20, 1920.

TUES., JUNE 29 — *The King accepts my ministry — I in the Int. Dep. — Creighton, For. Aff. — Kanoa, Finance — Dare, Atty. Gen. H. M. wanted to defer action till Saturday. I showed H. M. that treasury was empty — could only get accom[m]odation from Spreckels — must satisfy him. H. M. ordered me to issue commissions at once.*

JUNE 29. *I in the Interior Department.* Note that the reported cabinet proposals of the king (diary entries of June 26 and June 28) did not include Gibson, and that he was not appointed minister of foreign affairs. It seems clear that Gibson's power was waning.

WED., JUNE 30 — *Ten minutes at the Convent before 9 A.M.*
The new Ministry in their seats this morn. A sneer
about a "Spreckels Ministry."
Adj[ourned].

JUNE 30. *A "Spreckels Ministry."* The *Gazette* for July 5, among even more caustic criticisms, called the new cabinet "the sweepings of Spreckels' sugar refinery." On the floor of the legislature on Aug. 12, Rep. Dickey asked Gibson why, if he had such love for the Hawaiians, had he imported two ministers, Dare and Creighton, from California. Gibson answered that the choice of ministers was His Majesty's. Thurston then asked, "His Majesty Kalakaua or His Majesty Spreckels?" Gibson said this was a scandalous and insulting remark. *Pacific Commercial Advertiser*, Aug. 13, 1886.

SUN., JULY 11 — *Father Damien arrived at Kakaako. He is*
a confirmed leper — was advised not to come — but was
determined to visit the Sisters. I begin to doubt the
genuineness of his religious devotion.

MON., JULY 12 — *At the Convent this morning. S. M. and*
Sisters touched by the misfortune of the "noble priest" —
are deeply moved. I doubt not the genuineness of the
charity of S. M⁸ noble heart.

58

TUES., JULY 13 — *I sent Father Damien some wine & many things for his use and comfort. S. M. rewarded me with tender thanks. I called on Father D. — and still I have some misgivings — he talks too much.*

THURS., JULY 15 — *S. M. told me she was completely wearied out with Father Damien's talk — will be content when he returns to Molokai. He amused himself with the girls at the Home "like an old playmate."*

FRI., JULY 16 — *The King by my request called on Father Damien.*

Left per Likelike *for Kalaupapa at 9.30 P.M. Father Damien returns to Kalawao.*

JULY 16. *Father Damien returns to Kalawao*, Molokai. Damien's symptoms of leprosy had been visible in 1884. In March 1886, Dr. A. Mouritz, resident physician at the Molokai settlement, wrote Bishop Hermann to recommend that Damien go to Honolulu to take the Goto treatment of hot baths and other medicines. When Damien returned to the Molokai settlement, July 16, he said that he had felt homesick for that place and would try to establish the Goto treatment there. This was done, but the treatment was gradually abandoned because of side effects. A. Mouritz, *A Brief World History of Leprosy*, pp. 61–62.

SAT., JULY 17 — *An unsatisfactory reception by lepers at Kalawao — I feel that they have been prompted by the Opposition from Honolulu.*

Return to Honolulu by 6.30 P.M.

JULY 17. *Unsatisfactory reception by lepers.* The legislature
had appointed a committee of five to look into conditions
at Molokai. Gibson, not a member of the committee, went
presumably in his capacity as president of the board of
health. As such, he was technically in charge of the
settlement. He heard a great many complaints from the
lepers, and he made a speech in which he said: "I was
glad to see Father Damien, who came to town to see about
the Japanese doctor [Goto] and his method of treatment....
I believe that if he came here, he might do you a great deal
of good.... Yesterday His Majesty the King called on
Father Damien. This was not only a mark of His Majesty's
respect for the man who has given his life for you, but
also shows His Majesty's deep interest in your welfare."
Daily Bulletin, July 19, 1886. See also full accounts of the
visit in *Pacific Commercial Advertiser,* July 19, 1886;
Hawaiian Gazette, July 20, 1886. Over the years, Gibson
strove to improve the lot of the lepers. But theirs was a
miserable one, because little was known about the disease.
It was thus easy for the Opposition to make Gibson the
scapegoat.

SUN., JULY 18 — *With the King at noon. Afterwards called
on Mr Spreckels.*

At the Convent this P.M. *— a warm welcome back.*

MON., JULY 19 — *Drove with Talula and the children in
wagonette to the Convent.*

TUES., JULY 20 — *My state of health not very good — the
cough severe at times.*

At the Convent — S. M. comforts me.

*Capt Ira B. Dutton called — a religious enthusiast —
volunteers to assist at Leper Settlement.*

JULY 20. *Ira B. Dutton* (1843–1931) became a Catholic in 1883
and vowed to do charitable work the rest of his life because
of earlier sins of the flesh. Taking the name Brother Joseph

Dutton, he worked at the Molokai leper settlement from
1886 to 1931.

In his own account of the interview Dutton says he told
Gibson: "I have come here to go to Molokai and spend
the remainder of my life in work among the lepers."
Gibson asked him for a brief account of his past life. He
appeared to be satisfied that Dutton was in earnest and that
he was physically and otherwise able to take up the work.
Gibson was willing to offer pay for the work, but Dutton
would not consider taking any. He did not even allow
Gibson to pay his passage to Kalaupapa, Molokai, where he
arrived on July 29. *Joseph Dutton: His Memoirs*, ed.
Howard D. Case (Honolulu: Star-Bulletin, 1931), pp. 65–66.

WED., JULY 21 — *The King sent for me at 9 A.M. Very
cordial.*

THURS., JULY 22 — *Mr Dutton accompanied by Father
Sylvester called at Convent. He says he wants to do the
will of the "blessed Lord" by waiting on lepers.*

JULY 22. *Father Sylvester.* An assistant to Bishop Hermann;
also principal of St. Louis College, Honolulu (a boarding
school for boys, actually through high school level).
Honolulu Almanac and Directory, 1887, ed. R. J. Creighton
(Honolulu, 1887), pp. 30–31.

FRI., JULY 23 — *My foreign policy on trial in the House —
well vindicated by the vote of $30,000 for foreign missions.
At the Convent this aft. Dutton there again. He may
be genuine — but a good deal of cant about him.*

JULY 23. *$30,000 for foreign missions.* In debate with Thurston
about this item Gibson said it had been advantageous to

Hawaii to be represented at the coronation of the Russian
Czar. "It was so pleasing to the Emperor of Russia that
he commanded one of his ships of war to go to Hawaii
with a decoration ... worth $18,000 for His Majesty."
Hawaiian Hansard (Honolulu: Daily Bulletin, 1886), pp.
398–399. The *Daily Bulletin* of July 22 commented
editorially: "The mission cost the treasury in the vicinity
of $20,000, so that the net value of the compliment is ...
a clear loss of $2,000."

SUN., JULY 25 — *Attended mass at Cathedral 6* A.M.

MON., JULY 26 — *St Anna's Day — spent two hours very
happily at Kakaako.*
    Adjournment of the House till the 9th Aug.

JULY 26. *Adjournment of the House,* to permit those members
who were also tax assessors to return to their districts and
attend to their assessment duties. This gave the Opposition
party another chance to attack the practice of allowing
legislators to hold other government offices. *Daily Bulletin,*
July 27, 1886.

TUES., JULY 27 — *Talula, Fred and children attended by
Kahaulelio and Yamato, went to Lahaina per* Likelike.
    At Convent 6 P.M.

JULY 27. *Kahaulelio and Yamato.* Passenger list for *Likelike*
shows: "F. H. Hayselden, wife, 5 children and 2 servants."
Daily Bulletin, July 28, 1886.

WED., JULY 28 — *Mrs Strong preparing designs for insignia
of the new order of the Star of Oceania.*

At Convent 3 P.M. *Took Sr Rosalia a small bird in a cage.*

JULY 28. *Star of Oceania.* For photograph of insignia, see
G. Medcalf, *Hawaiian Royal Orders,* p. 42.

FRI., JULY 30 — *Great joy and delight at K — unexpected happiness.*
At St Louis school exhibition.
With Mr Spreckels this ev.

JULY 30. *St. Louis school exhibition.* Annual examinations
attended by Gibson (as president of the board of education)
and by many distinguished guests including the king and
Bishop Hermann Koeckemann. Gibson remarked that the
entertainment was inspiring; and that he saw evidence
of thorough training in solid education. The pupils should
appreciate not only their prizes, but also their able teachers.
Pacific Commercial Advertiser, July 31, 1886.

SAT., JULY 31 — *Farewell to Mr and Mrs and Miss Spreckels
on board the* Australia. *Interview of Spreckels and the
King before leaving — to maintain the present ministry.*
At the Convent 3 P.M.

JULY 31. *Departure of Spreckels.* The king, Princess
Liliuokalani, and Gibson were at the wharf. "Wreaths of
flowers and sweet-scented leaves entwined ... the necks
and shoulders of most of the passengers.... The Royal
Hawaiian Band ... played the steamer off in lively style."
Daily Bulletin, July 31, 1886. Spreckels' departure was
probably a tactical blunder in his campaign for economy

in government and for preventing loans from anyone but
himself.

MON., AUG. 2 — *Trouble at the Kapiolani Home. Seven
girls ran away. Came back again — but much trouble
with them. I flogged three of them.*

TUES., AUG. 3 — *The girls at Kapiolani Home again missing.
Active search all over town. I was at Home with Marshal
Kaulukou & two constables this ev. Distress of the
Mother and Sisters.*

AUG. 3. *John L. Kaulukou* had been appointed marshal on
July 31. Dole complained that he was now holding two
offices and that he should be ousted from the legislature.
Attorney General Dare said holding two offices was not in
conflict with the constitution. *Hawaiian Hansard*, p. 250.

WED., AUG 4 — *Discovery of girls — had never left the
premises — were stowed away under the house under
a stairway. An insane propensity in these girls brought
up in the lawless atmosphere of Kalawao.*

THURS., AUG. 5 — *Continued trouble with the girls. I had
one, Alapai, placed in solitary confinement. The
poor-dear Mother's trouble and anxiety.*

FRI., AUG. 6 — *This trouble with the girls at the Home is
most extraordinary. They seem untamable. They defy
the Sisters and yell for hours like fiends.*

AUG. 6. *Trouble with girls.* See also "Escaped from the Home," *Daily Bulletin*, Aug. 5, 1886.

SAT., AUG. 7 — *Return of Sr Benedicta.*

AUG. 7. *Return of Sr. Benedicta*, from Wailuku, Maui, on the *Likelike. Pacific Commercial Advertiser*, Aug. 9, 1886.

SUN., AUG. 8 — *At Mr Neumann's house. He intimated that he could prove the authorship of hostile articles in* Gazette *— Purvis. The King at my house — will remove Purvis & Judd too, if he has proof.*

Alameda *and* Zealandia *arrived.*

Sent dinner, roast duck &c to Convent.

AUG. 8. *Removal of Purvis and Judd.* Charles H. Judd resigned as chamberlain (and commissioner of crown lands) on Aug. 30. Curtis P. Iaukea replaced him. *Pacific Commercial Advertiser*, Aug. 31, 1886. Judd's resignation was requested "for certain improper conduct." Cabinet Council Minute Book, Aug. 30, 1886. He and Purvis were suspected of feeding derogatory information about the government to the *Gazette.*

Edward William Purvis, vice chamberlain, resigned soon after Judd. Purvis was a probable author or coauthor of two notorious burlesques on the Kalakaua regime: The *Grand Duke of Gynbergdrinkenstein* and *Gynberg Ballads.* R. S. Kuykendall, *The Hawaiian Kingdom, 1874–1893*, pp. 346–347.

MON., AUG. 9 — *The day went off well. Expected a good deal of work & bother. All right in the House. Met*

Mr Armstrong. The King said to me, we have no propositions to make to Mr A.

Twice at the Convent today.

AUG. 9. *Henry R. Armstrong,* a partner in the London firm of Skinner & Co., successors to A. Hoffnung & Co. Armstrong, at the instigation of Hoffnung, represented a London syndicate that wanted to float a Hawaiian government loan. R. S. Kuykendall, *The Hawaiian Kingdom, 1874–1893,* pp. 294–295.

No propositions to Armstrong. The king may have been trying to put Gibson off. In the next several days the king entertained Armstrong in grand style and was in turn entertained by him. Gibson was missing from these entertainments.

WED., AUG. 11 — *Hear that Geo. Macfarlane and Mr Neumann are stuffing the King with ideas about a London loan, through Mr Armstrong.*

At the Convent.

AUG. 11. *London loan.* On this same day Gibson said in the legislature he was "not now in favor of borrowing any money, except in the ordinary way from moneyed men in the country." This meant mainly Spreckels. *Hawaiian Hansard,* pp. 437–438.

SAT., AUG. 14 — *More about Armstrong and the English loans.*

At the Convent.

THURS., AUG. 19 — *Happiness at K.*

66

SAT., AUG. 21 — *Arrival of Miss Edith Turton to spend a few days with us.*

SUN., AUG. 22 — *Sent dinner to Convent — ducks and fresh apple pie.*

MON., AUG. 23 — *Lanai election discussion — anxious.*
The King at lunch.
Arrival of Australia. *Sent fruits — peaches, plums &c to Convent.*

AUG. 23. *Lanai election discussion.* On May 29 Thurston had introduced a resolution to investigate alleged threats against Lanai voters during the February legislative election. In effect he charged that Gibson, through his son Henry and his nephew Jesse Morehead, had threatened certain voters with loss of pasturage and fishing rights on Lanai. Gibson seconded the motion for an investigation. He claimed he had done nothing wrong and had nothing to hide. The investigating committee included three Opposition members and two Government members (Hayselden was one).

The committee presented two reports, strictly along party lines. These were discussed in the legislature on Aug. 23 and 24. The legislature adopted the minority report absolving Gibson.

The reports tell a good deal about the operations of Gibson's Lanai sheep ranch. Gibson said he had not been to Lanai since 1879, and that Hayselden was his general agent there and Irwin & Co. his business agents. He said his son Henry was a stockman and his nephew Jesse a foreman, and that they had no power to act in Gibson's name. *Daily Bulletin,* May 29, 1886; *Hawaiian Hansard,* pp. 509–511, 515–516; *Hawaiian Gazette,* Aug. 24, 1886; *Pacific Commercial Advertiser,* Aug. 25, 1886.

TUES., AUG. 24 — *A happy half hour at Kakaako.*
Triumph in the Assembly — 24 to 6.

The King at lunch.

Two runaway girls from Kapiolani Home captured and confined in Station House.

AUG. 24. *Triumph in the Assembly.* Adoption of the minority report of Lanai elections committee absolving Gibson. The vote was actually 24 to 7. *Hawaiian Hansard*, p. 516.

WED., AUG. 25 — *The King at lunch.*

I took the two girls out of Station House. Happiness with the dear Mother.

THURS., AUG. 26 — *Neumann and Macfarlane urging a new loan bill. I want to defer consideration. But the King has been prompted by Neumann to desire a credit in London.* ["He is tired of my leadership" scrawled out]

FRI., AUG. 27 — *Anxious to stave off consideration of loan bill.*

The King and Queen went to Kapiolani Home. I met them there at 11.30 A.M. An interesting visit ["self-denial" scrawled out]

SAT., AUG. 28 — *Taking a more satisfied view of the loan measure — if I can have passed the loan bill I introduced.*

MON., AUG. 30 — *The loan bill I introduced in May to be considered.*

TUES., AUG. 31 — *The Mother and Sister Crescentia called upon the English Sisters.*

Passage of loan bill — second reading.

AUG. 31. *Sister Crescentia* Eilers, one of the original group who arrived with Mother Marianne on Nov. 8, 1883. She was one of Marianne's chief assistants and usually in charge when the Mother was absent. L. V. Jacks, *Mother Marianne of Molokai*, pp. 19, 30, 43.

The English Sisters, the Devonport sisters (Episcopal) of St. Andrew's Priory, just north of the Palace. *Honolulu Almanac and Directory, 1887.*

WED., SEPT. 1 — *Final passage of the loan bill.*
At Kakaako.

SEPT. 1. *Passage of loan bill.* King Kalakaua signed the bill at once. Geo. W. Macfarlane left this same day for San Francisco with a copy of the bill. Before leaving, he conferred with Kalakaua aboard the *Australia.* Macfarlane was to confer with H. R. Armstrong in San Francisco. He was also to "explain" the loan bill to Spreckels and to try to mollify him. R. S. Kuykendall, *The Hawaiian Kingdom, 1874–1893*, p. 296; Jacob Adler, *Claus Spreckels, the Sugar King in Hawaii* (Honolulu: University of Hawaii Press, 1966), pp. 193–194.

THURS., SEPT. 2 — *At Kakaako.*

SEPT. 2. Gibson does not mention that he went to an elaborate forty-eighth birthday party for Princess (later Queen) Liliuokalani at her Palama residence.

During the party King Kalakaua proposed a toast to the ladies, and called on Neumann and Gibson to respond. Gibson said: "His Majesty has cast a reflection upon my

singleness of life and apparent want of appreciation of the
fair sex. But it is indeed my high appreciation, my unbounded
admiration for, and devotion to the fair sex, that has led to
my difficulty of choice." He praised Liliuokalani, concluding:
"And in honoring her, I desire to set forth how much I
honor the good amongst the sex which she so worthily
represents: I am happy to respond to this toast and fervently
say, the ladies, God bless them."

Along with many other gifts, the princess received from
Gibson a silver soup ladle. *Pacific Commercial Advertiser,*
Sept. 3, 1886.

SAT., SEPT. 4 — *Papa with a loving daughter at Kakaako.
Visit of English Sisters at my house.
Met Mr Greenbaum — Am. Consul at Samoa. I
recommended his appointment as Haw. Consul.*

SEPT. 4. *Berthold Greenbaum* [Greenebaum] soon got an
appointment as Hawaiian vice consul at Samoa, but nothing
ever came of it. Gibson was trying to tie Hawaii's policy
in Samoa to U.S. policy. But Greenebaum was out of favor
with all the powers in Samoa: Great Britain, Germany, and
even the United States. President Cleveland, in his Dec. 6,
1886, message to the U.S. Congress said that Greenebaum
had presumed to accept King Malietoa's offer to put
Samoa under U.S. protection. Cleveland went on: "The
proceeding was promptly disavowed, and the overzealous
official recalled." *Daily Bulletin,* Dec. 18, 1886; *Pacific
Commercial Advertiser,* Dec. 16, 1886; Jason Horn, "Primacy
of the Pacific under the Hawaiian Kingdom," master's thesis
(University of Hawaii, 1951), pp. 101–102.

SUN., SEPT. 5 — *Meeting of Cabinet at Palace. Moderate
views of the King in respect to temporary bond for loan.
Arrival of* Moskwa *— sent her out of harbor. Meeting
of Board of Health.*

SEPT. 5. *Moskwa sent out of harbor.* The Russian warship carried high-ranking officers, including Vice Admiral J. Shestakoff (or Chestakoff), minister of marine and aide-de-camp to the emperor. The ship had come from Yokohama where cholera had been reported. Doctors John Brodie and George Trousseau examined and fumigated the ship, which was then permitted to enter the harbor. *Daily Bulletin,* Sept. 6, 1886.

MON., SEPT. 6 — *A few sweet minutes at Br. H. this morning.*

The King at lunch.

TUES., SEPT. 7 — *At Kakaako half an hour this morning.*
The King at lunch.

WED., SEPT. 8 — *Departure Admiral Chestakoff. I gave him all Govt Dept reports & sanitary instructions.*

A cherry at Kakaako — Mr [a few words erased]
The King will be satisfied with rev. cutter instead of London loan.

SEPT. 8. *Revenue cutter.* The king's appetite for a ship may have been whetted by trips aboard the yacht *Brunhilde* (see diary entry of Sept. 16, 1886). On Sept. 27, Kaulukou introduced in the legislature an item of $100,000 for a yacht for the king. Thurston asked if Kaulukou were serious. Gibson said it would be useful for the government to have a revenue cutter to stop smuggling, to help disabled vessels, etc. (Gibson was doubtless also thinking of a ship to further Hawaii's policy of "Primacy of the Pacific.") A few days later the item passed. Representative Sanford B. Dole jeered that the ship was nothing but a royal play thing, and soon the members would be voting for a bicycle for His Majesty. *Pacific Commercial Advertiser,* Sept. 28, Oct. 2, 1886.

THURS., SEPT. 9 — *The King at lunch.*

FRI., SEPT. 10 — *The King at lunch.*
At Kakaako.

SAT., SEPT. 11 — *At the Convent and Home — so happy.*

MON., SEPT. 13 — *Neumann tells me that the King is galled at non-result of two million loan scheme. N. wants to make him feel so.*
K------ ["At Kakaako" erased]

SEPT. 13. *King galled at non-result of loan scheme.* Armstrong had left Honolulu on Aug. 28, before passage of the loan bill, and without making any commitment. The king knew of Spreckels' opposition to a loan in London. Eventually $1,000,000 was borrowed there, at great cost.

TUES., SEPT. 14 — *Reception at house of Mr Ando in honor of Capt Fukushima of* Tsukuba.

SEPT. 14. *Reception for Capt. Y. Fukushima of Japanese training frigate Tsukuba.* Elaborate affair described as the "social event of the season." Long account, with guest list, in *Pacific Commercial Advertiser*, Sept. 15, 1886.

WED., SEPT. 15 — *Talk with the King about the loan — he is easy on the subject — frank with me.*
K------ ["At Kakaako" erased]

THURS., SEPT. 16 — *Went on board* Tsukuba *in company with Creighton. Pleasantly received, but no salute. Surprise and enquiry — the King who was on board Yacht* Brunhildia *indignant, because no salute.*

K------ ["At Home and Kakaako" erased]

SEPT. 16. *No salute by Tsukuba.* It was reported that R. J. Creighton, foreign minister, protested in writing the failure to salute and then withdrew the correspondence in considerable embarrassment. *Hawaiian Gazette*, Sept. 21, 28, 1886.

Brunhildia [Brunhilde], a private yacht. The king was aboard at the invitation of Capt. J. J. Phelps, the owner, of Englewood, N.J. He was making a trip around the world. *Daily Bulletin*, Sept. 16, 1886; *Pacific Commercial Advertiser*, Sept. 17, 1886.

FRI., SEPT. 17 — *Explanations — Regulation of Jap[anese] navy that no official can be saluted whilst the Sovereign is in the harbor — but Capt Fukushima expressed regret he did not so inform ministers. All right.*

At Kakaako in new buggy with Talula.

SAT., SEPT. 18 — *On board the* Tsukuba *with the King and suite. Royal courtesies — tedious exercises, and an unsatisfactory lunch of wine, ice cream, cakes & fruits.*

At Kakaako for half an hour.

SEPT. 18. *Royal courtesies aboard Tsukuba.* The Japanese naval cadets manned the yards and put on a show of acrobatics aloft. The show lasted over two hours. *Daily Bulletin*, Sept. 18, 1886; *Pacific Commercial Advertiser*, Sept. 20, 1886.

SUN., SEPT. 19 — *Sent a bot. of wine and some flowers to Convent. Got a sweet note in return.*

Mr Creighton called in company with Mr J. J. Aubertin. Chat about Camoens and Prince Henry.

SEPT. 19. *John James Aubertin* (1818?–1900), author and traveler. He published two volumes of translations of poetry by Luís de Camoens (1524[?]–1580), Portuguese epic poet. Aubertin's *A Fight with Distances* (London, 1888) has a section on his trip to the Hawaiian Islands. *Modern English Biography*, ed. Frederic Boase, vol. 4, p. 202.

In *A Fight with Distances* Aubertin has recorded his impressions (pp. 192–196) of Gibson and Kalakaua. On Gibson: "What took me quite by surprise was to find him speaking of a small work [on Camoens] . . . which he had written . . . and a copy of which he produced and presented to me. . . . He was aware (but I know not how) that I had translated 'The Lusiads' . . . and thus I suddenly found myself, even in the Hawaiian Islands, talking of Camoens!"

On Kalakaua: "On Monday, the 20th, Mr. Gibson . . . presented me to his Majesty. . . . The first thing that struck me was that his Majesty had a very pleasant voice. . . . The next point was his Majesty's facile English; it ran without effort. . . . His Majesty conversed upon a variety of topics, showing much general knowledge and much diplomatic capacity. . . . [Next day he] showed me a large collection of maps, tracing his own workings out of the geographical genealogy of the islands. . . . He then . . . showed me a most beautiful spread of the old feather cloaks. . . . The art is lost, and the king told me he was making every possible effort to revive it. . . . So soon as I could take my eyes off these beautiful objects, his Majesty bid me accompany him to his Prime Minister's, where he was going to luncheon, and afterwards (which act of condescension I was bound to obey) drove me to the hotel."

Camoens and Prince Henry. Gibson had written newspaper articles about Camoens and about Prince Henry the

Navigator (1394–1460), Portuguese explorer. Both were among his special heroes.

THURS., SEPT. 30 — *The King proposes delay in final passage of amended loan act till* Mararoa *arrives — Ed Macfarlane has been suggesting to wait for his bro. George W. Macfarlane.*

FRI., OCT. 1 — *Much fatigued — nervous depression — prolonged session.*

SAT., OCT. 2 — *Arrival of* Mararoa — *and Mr Spreckels. No session. Satisfactory encounter — the King, Mr Spreckels and myself. Mr S. will take the loan. A happy hour at Kakaako.*

OCT. 2. *Spreckels arrives.* "Sir Claus had blood in his eye. I am told he spent two hours and a half in the palace on Sunday." *Hawaiian Gazette* columnist "Zip" in issue of Oct. 5, 1886. Geo. Macfarlane had been expected on the *Mararoa* and Spreckels' arrival was a surprise. He had come to look after his threatened interests as chief creditor of the Hawaiian kingdom.

MON., OCT. 4 — *Mr Spreckels perfectly satisfied with the affairs of the Govt and the state of the country. A happy hour with my child.*

OCT. 4. *My child* could mean daughter Talula, but more likely refers to Marianne.

WED., OCT. 6 — *Closing work of the appropriation bill — singing of the Assembly.*

 K------ ["At Kakaako" erased]

OCT. 6. *Singing of the Assembly.* The legislators were getting tired of the long session. Rep. Dickey enlivened final consideration of the appropriation bill by some "extravagantly absurd motions." Then the legislators "gave expression to their feelings . . . in singing several musical selections with great spirit and in excellent taste." *Pacific Commercial Advertiser*, Oct. 7, 1886.

THURS., OCT. 7 — *Arrival of Australia — Geo. W. Macfarlane. London loan played out. The King fully accepts propositions of Mr Spreckels. The King at lunch. At Kakaako this P.M.*

OCT. 7. *Arrival of Macfarlane.* This entry is puzzling. The *Australia* did not arrive until 5 A.M. on Saturday, Oct. 9. *Daily Bulletin*, Oct. 9, 1886; *Pacific Commercial Advertiser*, Oct. 10, 1886.

King at lunch. The lunch followed an audience in the throne room where a great many appointments were announced and decorations awarded. Appointments: Robert J. Creighton, secretary of war and of the navy (replaced one week later by Gibson himself); John O. Dominis, commander-in-chief of the armed forces; Curtis P. Iaukea, governor of Oahu, adjutant general of the armed forces, and private secretary to the king. Decorations: Claus Spreckels, grand officer of the order of Kapiolani; William G. Irwin, knight commander of the same order. At lunch Gibson led the toasts to the king, and to Dominis, among others. *Pacific Commercial Advertiser*, Oct. 8, 1886.

FRI., OCT. 8 — *Mr Spreckels proposes a restrictive amendment to loan bill which the King does not like — yet says he will accept.*

The King at lunch at my house.

SAT., OCT. 9 — *Arrival Sister Bonaventura. A happy hour at Kakaako.*

I regret that Mr Spreckels urges his restrictive amendment. The King at lunch.

K------ ["Happy — Kakaako" erased]

OCT. 9. *Restrictive amendment,* to give Spreckels' bonds priority, as to payment, over any bonds issued in London. Attorney General Dare pushed the amendment in the legislature. R. S. Kuykendall, *The Hawaiian Kingdom, 1874–1893,* pp. 296–298.

In the evening there was a big dinner at the home of Paul Neumann, honoring Wm. G. Irwin. The king was present, also Geo. Macfarlane, the Royal Hawaiian Band, and others. No mention of presence of Gibson. *Pacific Commercial Advertiser,* Oct. 11, 1886.

MON., OCT. 11 — *Threatening appearances — Mr Spreckels insists with offensive dictation to have his restrictive amendment to loan bill passed in the Assembly.*

WED., OCT. 13 — *Mr Spreckels with the King and Members at lunch at my house — offensive dictatorial talk of Mr S. — great offense to native Members — want to prove who is King.*

Adverse vote in the Assembly. Resignation of Ministers.

OCT. 13. *Adverse vote, resignation of ministers.* The vote was against the Spreckels amendment to the London loan bill. The cabinet then resigned. (This was a convenient way for Dare and Creighton, Spreckels' henchmen, to bow out.) Gibson and Kanoa were reappointed the next day.

THURS., OCT. 14 — *I accept office again with Aholo, Int. — Kanoa, Finance — and Kaulukou, Atty. Genl. Doing this against my better judgement.*

FRI., OCT. 15 — *Complete break of H. M. with Mr Spreckels.*

SAT., OCT. 16 — *Prorogation of the Legislature.*

OCT. 16. Gibson does not mention his presence at a birthday luau for Princess Kaiulani at the home of her parents A. S. Cleghorn and Princess Likelike. Gibson presented a gift of $10 in gold coins. *Pacific Commercial Advertiser,* Oct. 18, 1886.

SUN., OCT. 17 — *Enna Dudoit came to pay me a visit.*

OCT. 17. *Enna Dudoit,* Adrienne Blanche Dudoit, daughter of Anna Dudoit who was the widow of one-time French consul in Honolulu, Jules Dudoit.

FRI., OCT. 22 — *Meeting of King and Ministers at lunch at my house. Determination of King to send Geo. W. Macfarlane to London to negotiate loan. Dare offers in name of Spreckels to take up all the loan, but not listened to.*

Happy at Kakaako.

OCT. 22. Spreckels returned all his royal decorations to the office of the king's chamberlain. *Hawaiian Gazette*, Oct. 26, 1886.

SAT., OCT. 23 — *Departure of Mr Spreckels per* Mariposa *without reconciliation. The King's unaccountable favor to Geo. W. Macfarlane. I gave to George letter of introduction to Mrs Maberly.*

Annoying event at Kakaako — I am afraid I am becoming tiresome.

OCT. 23. *King's favor to Macfarlane.* He appointed Macfarlane financial agent to negotiate the loan in London. H. R. Armstrong received a similar appointment. "By Authority," *Pacific Commercial Advertiser*, Oct. 23, 1886. Ironically, Macfarlane left for San Francisco on the same boat with Spreckels. Gibson had an interview with Macfarlane at the wharf.

Letter to Mrs. Maberly. She may have had some connection with the Court of St. James. See Tanner address in Addresses, 1886 Diary, and corresponding note.

SUN., OCT. 24 — *Miss Enna at the house.*

MON., OCT. 25 — *At Kakaako — all happy again. My misunderstanding.*

The King and Ministers Aholo and Kanoa at my house to lunch — to consider the state of the finances.

Sala Rossini called. He arrived per Mariposa.

OCT. 25. *Signor Giuseppe Sala Rossini,* a sculptor, "well advanced in years." He did a Civil War memorial in West Roxbury, Mass., and allegorical figures for the Buffalo, N.Y., customs house. In Hawaii he hoped to recover his health. He fitted up a studio on Fort Street. *Pacific Commercial Advertiser,* Dec. 7, 1886.

TUES., OCT. 26 — *The King and Ministers at my house to lunch. Conference to consider requirements of departments.*

Happy jaunt to Park and ravine beyond with S. M. and Sr Bonaventura. Got plants at Government nursery.

WED., OCT. 27 — *I arranged with Robinson and Allen to take $160,000 in bonds.*

At Kakaako.

OCT. 27. *Robinson and Allen.* Mark P. Robinson and Samuel C. Allen were partners in the building materials firm of Allen and Robinson. The Cabinet Council Minute Book of Oct. 19, 1886, mentions an offer by *trustees of the Robinson estate* to take $100,000 of new bonds and also an additional amount equal to the bonds held by them.

THURS., OCT. 28 — *Robinson exchanged $90,000 old bonds for new 6 per cents and bought for cash to amount of $70,000 less commission and interest.*

K------ ["Happy — Kakaako" erased]

SAT., OCT. 30 — *A delightful jaunt to Manoa valley with S. M. and Sister Bonaventura. Scrambling in the thicket — got a variety of ferns.*

OCT. 30. *Got a variety of ferns.* See Gibson's letter of Oct. 20, 1874, in which he wrote to a Miss Mosely of Honolulu that he was sending her ferns for her collection: "Some people make a business of fern collecting, but I am simply an amateur collector for pleasure; — and am only too happy to meet a young student or collector like yourself who will permit me to contribute a trifle for . . . amusement and instruction." Letter at Hawaiian Historical Society, Honolulu.

SUN., OCT. 31 — *At Kakaako a little while.*

MON., NOV. 1 — *Fred's birthday.*
   At Br. H.

NOV. 1. *Fred's birthday.* Talula's husband, Fred Harrison Hayselden (*b.* 1851), not her son Fred "Dada" Howard Hayselden (*b.* May 1, 1879).

TUES., NOV. 2 — *At Br. H.*

WED., NOV. 3 — *At Br. H.*

NOV. 3. *At Br. H.* "The Royal Hawaiian Band played . . . much to the delight and amusement of the inmates." *Pacific Commercial Advertiser*, Nov. 4, 1886.

THURS., NOV. 4 — *Little Lucy's birthday — now nine years of age.*

At Br. H.

NOV. 4. *Little Lucy's birthday.* Talula Lucy Gibson Hayselden, born Nov. 4, 1877. See Memoranda, 1886 Diary.

FRI., NOV. 5 — *Expect two new Sisters of Charity — Srs Cyrille and Irene.*

At Br. H.

NOV. 5. *Expect two new Sisters.* In a letter about travel expenses for them, Gibson had written: "I beg to say to you dear Madam that the Government and people of this Country appreciate the mission of charity to these islands, of Mother Marianne and her associate Sisters, as a blessing of incalculable value. — Our King and Queen hold the noble Sisterhood in the highest estimation. Therefore you and your Sisters in Syracuse may rest assured, that we will welcome any newcomers from your community with very glad hearts." Gibson to Mother Delphina of St. Anthony's Convent, Syracuse, N.Y., Aug. 27, 1886. Archives of Franciscan Sisters, Syracuse, N.Y.

SAT., NOV. 6 — *Meeting of Privy Council. My anxiety to have considered a charter for my Sisters of Charity. Passed the Council. A happy hour at Kakaako.*

Received from San Fran. two large elephant tusks — my present for the King on his birthday.

NOV. 6. *Charter for Sisters.* The petition, signed by Mother Marianne, was for a charter for a charitable institution

to be known as "The Third Franciscan Order." Privy
Council Minutes, Nov. 6, 1886, Archives of Hawaii.

SUN., NOV. 7 — *With my colleagues at the Palace — more*
pardons.

MON., NOV. 8 — *A very happy day — got the charter for*
Franciscan Sisters all completed. Took it to Kakaako —
a delightful afternoon. Commemoration of the
"Landing of the Sisters."

NOV. 8. *Landing of the Sisters.* This was the third anniversary
of Mother Marianne's arrival with six other Franciscan
sisters.

Gibson wrote to Sister Bonaventura (?) at the Convent
of St. Anthony on Maui: "I dare say you have not been
unmindful of the anniversary which the above date
indicates — 'The Landing of the Sisters' — that precious
pioneer band of Charity — and the precious volunteers
who followed them — God bless them all. I love and
honor them with my whole soul. I commemorated the
anniversary today. I accomplished a long desired purpose in
behalf of your Sisters in getting passed through the Privy
Council a Charter . . . which was signed and sealed today.
You are now a corporate institution of beneficence." Nov. 8,
1886, Archives of Franciscan Sisters, Syracuse, N.Y.

TUES., NOV. 9 — *The King very genial — enthusiastic about*
immigration of Javanese.

A disappointing visit at Kakaako.

Spear mounting the tusks with silver bands and
inscriptions.

NOV. 9. *Immigration from Java.* Immigration from Indonesia, of races "cognate with the Hawaiian," had been for almost a quarter of a century one of Gibson's pet aims. On Nov. 22 the Cabinet Council authorized him to correspond with the Dutch government about possible immigration to Hawaii from the Dutch East Indies. Cabinet Council Minute Book, Nov. 22, 1886. Nothing came of this.

Spear, John A., jeweler and engraver.

WED., NOV. 10 — *Down today. Saw my friends of Kakaako in town — disappointed.*

After a while a pleasant note. At Kakaako in the aft. — happy again.

Privy Council. Rossini's bust of Victor Emmanuel arrived per J. D. Spreckels.

THURS., NOV. 11 — *C. E. Williams making stand for elephant's tusks.*

Privy Council in For. Of. Bust of Victor Emmanuel set up in my hall.

NOV. 11. *C. E. Williams*, furniture dealer, upholsterer, embalmer, and undertaker.

FRI., NOV. 12 — *At Br. H. this morning. A pleasant hour — but must study contentment.*
Privy Council in For. Of.

SAT., NOV. 13 — *Sisters Bonaventura & Rosalia arrived per* Likelike. *At Br. Hospital.*

A happy afternoon at Br. H.

SUN., NOV. 14 — *Sent roast turkey &c to Convent of St Francis for their dinner today.*

MON., NOV. 15 — *Saw the King about order of precedence. Privy Council postponed.*

M. unwell. Saw her for a few minutes in parlor.

TUES., NOV. 16 — *Grand reception at Palace. Triumph of the King. No Fort St Church people there — but his own people in full force — a great day. My tusks especially honored.*

At Kakaako 4 P.M.

NOV. 16. *Fort Street Church*, Congregational, at Fort and Beretania streets, Honolulu, one of the forerunners of today's Central Union Church. The "Fort Street Church people" would include non-native residents who were shocked at the "recrudescence of heathenism" under the Kalakaua regime.

Tusks honored. A member of the king's staff — he must have been a strapping fellow — carried the tusks on a velvet cushion and preceded the king into the throne room. The tusks, mounted on a koa wood stand, each weighed more than fifty pounds. A silver tablet between them bore on one side the inscription: "His Majesty King Kalakaua, born November 16, 1836, ascended the throne of Hawaii, February 12, 1874. In commemoration of the fiftieth birthday of His Majesty." On the other side: "The horns of the righteous shall be exalted."

Among other gifts to the king at an elaborate *hookupu* (ceremonial paying of tribute) were fifty $20 gold pieces from the board of health, of which Gibson was president. Fred H. Hayselden, secretary of the board, made the presentation speech. Mrs. Hayselden, Gibson's daughter, presented a kukui nut watch chain and locket with portrait. *Pacific Commercial Advertiser*, Nov. 16, 17, 1886. *Hawaiian Gazette*, Nov. 23, 1886. *Honolulu Almanac and Directory*, 1887, p. 61.

◆§1886§◆

WED., NOV. 17 — *Arrival of two Sisters of Charity per Zealandia — Sisters Cyrilla and Irene — German. Sent by Father Schaefer from Providence, Lyons, France.*

I waited on M. and Sr Bonaventura at the steamer wharf till 8.30 P.M.

NOV. 17. *Father Boniface Schaefer*, missionary and director of the German Church, Lyons, France. See Addresses, 1886 Diary.

THURS., NOV. 18 — *Constant rain all day. Got trunk of newly arrived Sisters, and took it to Convent. Happy with M.*

FRI., NOV. 19 — *Rain all day.*

Interview with George W. Macfarlane at Palace in presence of Cabinet. Portuguese immigration the ruling idea of his friends in London, Skinner & Co.

NOV. 19. *Interview with Macfarlane.* He had returned from San Francisco on Nov. 17, possibly to report on cable communications with Skinner & Co. about the proposed loan and about Portuguese immigration. The cabinet decided to obtain information about the number of immigrants needed. Cabinet Council Minute Book, Nov. 19, 1886. Macfarlane left for England on Nov. 23. *Pacific Commercial Advertiser*, Nov. 23, 1886.

SAT., NOV. 20 — *Continued rain.*

Historical procession — at Palace. A happy hour at Kakaako. Geo. Macfarlane with me this evening.

NOV. 20. *Historical procession,* a part of the king's jubilee, had been held up for a few days by rain. It started at King and Nuuanu streets and ended at the Palace. Headed up by the Royal Hawaiian Band, the procession included floats with canoes and warriors in ancient costume, hula dancers, and, bringing up the rear, the Reform School band. One float illustrated a way of fishing. The fishermen in loin cloths threw out a large seine and netted a few hefty Hawaiians. Accounts in *Daily Bulletin,* Nov. 20, 1886; *Pacific Commercial Advertiser,* Nov. 22, 1886; *Hawaiian Gazette,* Nov. 30, 1886.

SUN., NOV. 21 — *Continued rain.*

MON., NOV. 22 — *A happy hour at Br. H.*

TUES., NOV. 23 — *Luau at Palace.*

Much fatigued — troublesome tooth.

At 4.30 left Palace and drove to wharf. Bid goodbye to Sister Bonaventura. Saw M. in carriage but did not join her. Fathers Leonor and Theodore on board.

NOV. 23. *Luau at Palace,* part of jubilee celebration. A lanai about 300 feet long by 30 feet wide had been built along the front of the palace, which was opened for inspection. The royal family received within the palace and gifts were displayed. About 1500 persons were served in three shifts. The menu: pig, raw and cooked, dried fish, crab, shrimp, seaweed, *awa* (a mildly narcotic drink), chicken, turkey, duck, poi, sweet potatoes, bananas, oranges, champagne, ale, and soda water. Hula dancing began in the evening and went on far into the night. *Pacific Commercial Advertiser,* Nov. 24, 1886.

Sister Bonaventura was returning to Malulani Hospital, Maui.

Father Leonor, an assistant to Bishop Hermann. After correspondence between Gibson and Bishop Hermann in 1883, Father Leonor had been commissioned to find sister-nurses for the Hawaiian lepers. "After arduous, and for a long time baffling endeavors in his many applications to the various religious orders in the United States, he found at last, after petitioning over fifty different religious Sisterhoods, a favorable hearing at the Franciscan Convent of Saint Anthony" in Syracuse, N.Y. "Gibson's Address" in *Dedication of Kapiolani Home* (Honolulu, 1885), pp. 9–10.

Father Theodore, pastor of a Catholic church on Maui. McKenney's *Hawaiian Directory*, 1885.

WED., NOV. 24 — *At Kakaako 10 A.M.*

M. Feer's absurd attitude about Fr. flag not being seen at Luau.

Writing notes for address on Independence Day.

NOV. 24. *French flag not seen.* At the luau, the wall behind the king was decorated with a large royal standard. The British flag was on his right, the U.S. flag on his left. *Pacific Commercial Advertiser*, Nov. 24, 1886.

Independence Day. On Nov. 28, 1843, in London, Great Britain and France signed a joint recognition of Hawaii's independence. As a matter of policy, the United States did not join in this but in the next year made a separate statement recognizing Hawaii's independence. Nov. 28 became a holiday of the kingdom. R. S. Kuykendall and A. Grove Day, *Hawaii: a History* (New York: Prentice-Hall, 1948), pp. 68–69.

THURS., NOV. 25 — *The Princess Lydia gave me Dr Hyde's letter declining to allow Kawaiahao school [to] attend birthday reception of King.*

K------ ["At Kakaako" scrawled out]

NOV. 25. *Princess Lydia Liliuokalani* (1838–1917), King

Kalakaua's sister. She became queen in 1891 and was deposed in the revolution of 1893.

Dr. Charles M. Hyde's letter. He was a trustee of Kawaiahao Female Seminary (on King Street, opposite Kawaiahao Church) where "mental and moral requirements of the girls are met, their characters developed and their young years permeated with influences calculated to qualify them to take their places in the domestic, social and religious departments of life." *The Friend,* February 1887, p. 9. Presumably he did not want the girls corrupted by such goings-on as the lascivious hula. This is the same Dr. Hyde whom Robert Louis Stevenson later castigated for a letter about Father Damien.

Gibson does not mention the state ball on the eve of this date. The lanai or veranda of the palace was decorated with ferns, evergreens, and flowers. Halfway up the lanai on either side were J. D. Strong's paintings of Honolulu harbor in 1836 and in 1886. (These pictures, each about 4 feet by 8 feet, are now in the reading room of the Archives of Hawaii.) The first dance was the Royal Quadrille. The king danced with Princess Liliuokalani, and Gibson with Mrs. Luther Aholo, wife of the minister of interior. *Daily Bulletin,* Nov. 26, 1886; *Hawaiian Gazette,* Nov. 30, 1886.

FRI., NOV. 26 — *Revising address — "Progress of Hawaii since 1836."*

NOV. 26. *Address, "Progress of Hawaii,"* delivered on Nov. 28 at Kaumakapili Church, the leading church of the Hawaiian people. The king was there, and the church was jammed full. Luther Aholo spoke first, in Hawaiian. Gibson then traced the progress of Hawaii in the fifty years since Kalakaua's birth, from weakness and poverty to strength and prosperity. Gibson said in part: "Fifty years ago the tide flowed where now are some of our busiest streets; a small coasting schooner anchored where now may be seen steam vessels carrying the Hawaiian flag across the ocean. . . . Kalo patches and grass huts, unshaded by any tree, except where the cocoanut fringed the shore, have been replaced by substantial buildings and busy streets, and the whole shaded by such a wealth of lovely foliage . . . busy haunts of

89

a commerce . . . brought with rapid strides to its present
high condition by the wise and patriotic effort of the King
whose jubilee we now celebrate." During the speech
Gibson used the king's full name: David Laamea
Kamanakapuu Mahinulani Naloiaehuokalani Lumialani
Kalakaua. The speech, one of Gibson's most eloquent, is
reported in four columns of the *Pacific Commercial
Advertiser*, Nov. 29, 1886.

SAT., NOV. 27 — *Departure per* W. G. Hall — *Talu[l]a,
Fred, all the children, and Meamatau, at 10* A.M.

NOV. 27. *Departure of Hayselden family*, for Lahaina. Fred
Hayselden may have gone to assist the Government party
candidate, Kia Nahaolelua, in a special election to replace
Representative Luther Aholo who had become a cabinet
member. Nahaolelua was elected on Dec. 6. A day or so
before the election, Hayselden gave an elaborate dinner at
Gibson's Lahaina residence, *Lanikeha. Pacific Commercial
Advertiser*, Dec. 14, 1886.

SUN., NOV. 28 — [*"Miss (Mrs?) Wodehouse called" erased*]

MON., NOV. 29 — *Excursion for Sisters and children of K.
Home to the house at the Park — M. and Sisters
Martha, Charles, Cyrilla & Irene — 11 girls — a run on
the Diamond Head slopes — a delightful day.
State dinner at the Palace.*

NOV. 29. *State dinner*. It was an elaborate formal affair in the
grand dining room of the palace. Mrs. J. D. Strong painted
the menus and place cards, which took a month of work.
Gibson's card had figures representing Politics, Health, and

Education. In one corner of the card was a sketch of a shepherd with crook. (Gibson owned a sheep ranch on Lanai.) After dinner there was dancing to the music of the Royal Hawaiian Band. Full column account in *Pacific Commercial Advertiser*, Nov. 30, 1886.

TUES., NOV. 30 — *At Br. H. in the morning — again in the afternoon. Commenced work with carpenters. M. called on Mother Judith.*

    Mrs Howard called.

NOV. 30. *Mrs. Howard called.* Mrs. Flora Howard St. Clair, a widow, who with her sister Alice Waite had come to Honolulu in February 1886. The sisters worked as book agents. Mrs. St. Clair sold some books to Gibson and became friendly with him. The degree of friendship later became a matter of dispute.

WED., DEC. 1 — *Dr Whitney inserted a fore-fronth* [sic] *tooth on pivot.*

    At Br. H.

DEC. 1. *John Morgan Whitney* practiced dentistry in Honolulu for more than fifty years beginning in 1869. *Men of Hawaii* (Honolulu, 1921), p. 421.

Fore-fronth tooth seems to be a weak attempt at humor.

THURS., DEC. 2 — *With M. this aft.*

SAT., DEC. 4 — *With M. this aft.*
Mrs Wodehouse called.

DEC. 4. *Mrs. James H. Wodehouse,* wife of British commissioner
and consul general.

SUN., DEC. 5 — *Went to Mass at 10 A.M. Sent dinner to the
Convent — a sweet note.*

MON., DEC. 6 — *M attended a school exhibition at school of
Sacred Hearts.*
  *A sudden and painful attack of diarrhoea this
morning.*
  *Loaned Mrs Wodehouse three hundred dollars to assist
her daughter Maud.*

DEC. 6. *Loan to Mrs. Wodehouse,* to help daughter Maud
with passage to Chile and marriage there to Robert S.
Lambert on Mar. 26, 1887. Maud and brother Guy left
Honolulu on Jan. 16, 1887. *Pacific Commercial Advertiser,*
Jan. 15, 17, 1887; *Hawaiian Gazette,* Jan. 18, 1887.

TUES., DEC. 7 — *The diarrhoea attacked me again last night.
Keeping in doors.*
  *Went to Br. H. this afternoon — both of us ailing
— a little out of sorts.*

WED., DEC. 8 — *Saw H. M. about Star of Oceania. Makes
me Chancellor.*

Paying off Spreckels. Told Giffard, Spreckels' interests cared for same as if our best friend.

Music at Kakaako. Dare there. A prayer and a vow — very happy — with M.

DEC. 8. *Walter M. Giffard,* chief clerk of Wm. G. Irwin & Co. (Spreckels and Irwin).

Music at Kakaako, a concert by the Royal Hawaiian Band. *Daily Bulletin,* Dec. 8, 1886.

THURS., DEC. 9 — *Another very happy day at Kakaako.*

FRI., DEC. 10 — *Wilson, Sup^t water works, drove me to receiving reservoir — a pleasant place — got some ferns.*

DEC. 10. *Charles B. Wilson,* superintendent of water works and also fire chief. In 1891 he became marshal of the kingdom and a member of the privy council. Index of Officeholders, Archives of Hawaii. He was the father of John H. Wilson who served four terms as mayor of Honolulu beginning in 1946.

SAT., DEC. 11 — *Took another trip to water works receiving reservoir to collect more ferns. A* [incomplete]

SUN., DEC. 12 — *Sent dinner to the Convent — pleasant thanks.*

MON., DEC. 13 — *Preparing instructions for Bush-Samoan mission.*

At Kakaako. My office undergoing renovation — no place for a tête à tête — disappointed. Letters to Talula, Fred, Lucy and Walter. Mr and Mrs Hendry with me this P.M.

DEC. 13. *Bush-Samoan mission.* The instructions dated Dec. 24, 1886, called for a mission of "friendship and courtesy" to Chief Malietoa from King Kalakaua. Bush was to try to reconcile rebellious chiefs (the strongest of these was Tamasese, favored by the Germans) to Chief Malietoa. Bush was to explore the possibility of an alliance between Hawaii and Samoa which would give Hawaii authority to speak to foreign powers on behalf of Samoan independence. R. S. Kuykendall, *The Hawaiian Kingdom, 1874–1893,* p. 325. Considering that Germany, Great Britain, and the United States were all jockeying for position in Samoa, Gibson's instructions might be described as not lacking in boldness.

TUES., DEC. 14 — *The King at the house. He there met Rossini. H. M. wants to take steps to purchase electric light plant for the city.*

Sent apples to Sister Bonaventura. At Kakaako — all right again. Sent breakfast to the Convent this morn. — 7 A.M.

DEC. 14. *Electric light plant.* Use of electric lights at the palace for the king's fiftieth birthday jubilee had stirred up interest. Honolulu streets were lit by electricity in 1888. See editorial "The Electric Light," *Pacific Commercial Advertiser,* Dec. 4, 1886, a sample of many contemporary editorials on the subject.

WED., DEC. 15 — *Called on Fanny Bickerton this forenoon.*
Arrival of Australia.
With M. this P.M.

THURS., DEC. 16 — *Letter of Carter about London loan —*
serious — work of Spreckels. The King determined. I
will furnish news for associated press to correct newspaper
lies.
A happy hour with M.
Cabinet meeting 6 P.M. — *organize Star of Oceania.*

DEC. 16. *News to correct newspaper lies.* The cabinet council
authorized Gibson to spend $300 a month for "publication
of correct information about this Kingdom in the press
of foreign countries." This was to correct such things as
reports by Spreckels that Hawaii was bankrupt, and
other reports to the effect that the Hawaiian kingdom was
for sale, England had a lien on all its revenues, and so forth.

Star of Oceania. The award was to be for "distinguished
services rendered to Us or to Our State and in advancing
the name and influence of Hawaii amongst the native
communities of the Islands of the Pacific and Indian Oceans,
and on contiguous continents." Full dress uniform of the
order included "a black dress coat, with the cuffs and . . .
collar trimmed with green and gold cord; white satin vest
. . . knee breeches; garters ornamented with gems; black silk
stockings; patent leather slippers; a court rapier . . . and
court chapeau without plume." *Hawaii Government Gazette,*
Feb. 7, 1887.
Gibson does not mention taking part in a presentation to
Kalakaua of the insignia and cordon of the Royal Order of
Kalakaua, of which the king himself was Grand Master.
The insignia, gift of the military forces of the kingdom,
contained 466 diamonds, and also some opals and rubies.
Daily Bulletin, Dec. 16, 1886; *Pacific Commercial Advertiser,*
Dec. 17, 1886.

1886

SAT., DEC. 18 — *Arranging for Bush to go to Samoa.*

SUN., DEC. 19 — *Feeling very well. Sent nice dinner to the Convent. Happy to gratify the good sisters.*

MON., DEC. 20 — *Cabinet meeting — disposal of lands — adjourn till tomorrow. Cabinet interference with Departmental work — the whole work of Govt. concentrated in the Palace.*
Letters to Talula & children. A happy hour at Kakaako.

DEC. 20. *Government concentrated in Palace.* Frequent cabinet changes, and interference by the king, caused trouble in the work of the departments. Gibson himself seems to have tried to keep too many reins in his own hands. He was often called "minister of everything."

TUES., DEC. 21 — *Cabinet meeting — disposal of lands. The dummy ministers.*
A happy hour with M. Sent bedsteads and other things to Sisters at Wailuku.

WED., DEC. 22 — *Rain all forenoon. Departure of* Australia. *I had to arrange every detail for work of Interior and Finance.*
At Kakaako.
Will send Strong to Samoa. Getting things for Christmas gifts to lepers. Mrs Howard called.

THURS., DEC. 23 — *Kanoa reduces Fred's rate for assessing from 4 to 3 per ct — a mean jealous native move.*

Christmas preparations. At Kakaako — a subdued feeling.

DEC. 23. *Kanoa reduces Fred's rate.* Fred Hayselden was tax assessor for Honolulu, besides being a member of the legislature.

FRI., DEC. 24 — *Getting things for the Branch Hospital and K. Home.*

A few nice presents — a handsome carriage rug from Maggie — large vases from Aki.

DEC. 24. *Aki.* Doubtless the same Tong Aki who lost $71,000 in an attempt to buy an opium license that had been authorized by the 1886 legislature. See also diary entries of Jan. 20 and Apr. 29, 1887.

SAT., DEC. 25 — *Rather a handsome get-up for the lepers at Kakaako. I distributed the gifts. Took lunch in the little office. A happy hour with M.*

SUN., DEC. 26 — *Tired out with yesterday's excitement — I must drop down a while.*

DEC. 26. In his weariness, Gibson does not even mention the departure of the Samoan mission aboard the *Zealandia:* J. E. Bush, ambassador to Samoa; H. F. Poor, secretary of legation; J. D. Strong, artist and collector. Gibson, with J. S. Webb, secretary of the foreign office, drove down to the

97

wharf early in the morning to see the mission off. *Daily Bulletin*, Dec. 27, 1886.

MON., DEC. 27 — *Cabinet meeting — appointment of Bickerton and Fornander as judges of Supr [eme] Court. At Kakaako this afternoon — not animated. Bickerton and his wife spent the evening with me.*

DEC. 27. *Appointment of Bickerton and Fornander.* This increased the membership of the supreme court from three to five, as provided by an act of the 1886 legislature. One reason for the act was that the justices also sat on circuit courts and were overburdened with cases. R. S. Kuykendall, *The Hawaiian Kingdom, 1874–1893*, p. 301.

Richard F. Bickerton (1844–1895) was being moved up from police and district judge for Honolulu. He had been a member of the legislature in 1878, the first in which Gibson served. In October 1887, he was to preside at a breach of promise suit against Gibson.

Abraham Fornander (1812–1887) was being moved up from the Maui circuit court. He is best remembered for his writings on Hawaiian traditions and lore. See his *Account of the Polynesian Race*, 3 vols. (London, 1878–1885).

TUES., DEC. 28 — *With M. a while this morning — occupied with her charges. I have but a secondary place.*

WED., DEC. 29 — *A Southern blow — heavy rain. Audience at Palace — Capt Goni — Chilⁿ man-o-war. Caught fresh cold — bad state of bowels.*
  Mrs Howard called. Did not go out.

DEC. 29. *Capt. Luis A. Goni* of the Chilean training corvette
Pilcomayo, which arrived in Honolulu on Dec. 26 from
Valparaiso. *Hawaiian Gazette,* Dec. 28, 1886.

THURS., DEC. 30 — *Unwell all day — soreness in the bowels.*

FRI., DEC. 31 — *Still unwell — but attended in full
uniform the Queen's reception at the Palace. Excused
my self at 12 o'clock.*

*On returning to house, met S. M. and Sister Crescentia
in their carriage — a ple[a]sant five minutes with them.
At 4 P.M. went to the Convent though suffering a
good deal — petted and nursed by M. and took tea there.
At home by 7 P.M.*

DEC. 31. *Queen's reception.* Queen Kapiolani (1834–1899) was
celebrating her fifty-second birthday. She was two years
older than Kalakaua.

Memoranda, 1886 Diary

M [arianne] born Jany 23ᵈ 1838.

Maggie Walker born Mar. 17. 1867.

Walter Hooulu Hayselden
born Feb. 20ᵗʰ 1876.

Talula Lucy Gibson Hayselden
born Nov. 4. 1877.

Frederick Howard Hayselden
born May 1. 1879 (Dada).

David Kanaiaupuni Hayselden
born June 11 [1882].

Henry Claus Hayselden
born [Oct. 7, 1883.] Died Dec [20] 1884.

Rachel Kuliakanuu Hayselden
born July 27. 1885.

Notes to Memoranda

MOTHER MARIANNE, born 1838. More likely 1836. See L. V. Jacks, *Mother Marianne of Molokai* (N.Y., 1935), pp. 190–192.

MAGGIE [MARGARET JANE] WALKER, daughter of John S. Walker.

WALTER HOOULU HAYSELDEN, died Mar. 29, 1949. His middle name means "to make grow," possibly related to *Hooulu Lahui,* "increase and preserve the nation," a motto of the Kalakaua-Gibson regime.

TALULA LUCY GIBSON HAYSELDEN, died May 1, 1933.

FREDERICK HOWARD HAYSELDEN, died Mar. 13, 1955.

DAVID KANAIAUPUNI ("AUPUNI") HAYSELDEN, born June 11, 1882, died Sept. 11, 1936. His middle name means "calm nation." Ironically, he was named after David Kalakaua, whose regime was hardly calm. Obituary, *Honolulu Advertiser,* Sept. 12, 1936; *Honolulu Star-Bulletin,* Sept. 14, 1936.

HENRY CLAUS HAYSELDEN, born Oct. 7, 1883, died Dec. 20, 1884. *The Friend,* February 1885. He was named after Claus Spreckels.

RACHEL KULIAKANUU HAYSELDEN married Wren W. Wescoatt at Lahaina Sept. 19, 1905. *The Friend,* Oct. 1905, p. 15. Her middle name comes from Queen Kapiolani's motto, "to strive for the summit." See *kūlia* in Pukui-Elbert, *Hawaiian Dictionary* (Honolulu: University of Hawaii Press, 1971). Rachel died May 24, 1972.

Addresses, 1886 Diary

NAME.   *Revd Mother Delphina*
STREET, NO.   *Convent St Anthony*
CITY.   *Syracuse N. Y.*

NAME.   *Revd Mother Marianne*
STREET, NO.   *Convent St Francis*
CITY.   *Honolulu H. I.*

NAME.   *Miss Tanner, c/o Mrs Maberly*
STREET, NO.   *no 13 Oakl[e]y St Chelsea*
CITY.   *S. W. London, England*

NAME.   *Randolph C. Want*
STREET, NO.   *Sol^r for Govt of N. S. W.*
CITY.   *5 Westminster. Chamber*
          Victoria St, London

NAME.   *Rev Father Boniface Schaefer*
STREET, NO.   *Missionary & Director of the*
                German Church
CITY.   *Rue Vendome 141, Lyons, France*

NAME.   *Mrs Elinor Gibson*

STREET, NO.   *Navesink, P. O. Monmouth Cy*

CITY.   *New Jersey*

NAME.   *Dr Wm. H. Robb*

STREET, NO.   *Amsterdam, Montgomery Cy*

CITY.   *G. H. Munson New York*

NAME.   *Mrs. Lucy T. Millie*

STREET, NO.   *689 Broadway*

CITY.   *New York City*

NAME.   *Joseph E. Gaunder*

STREET, NO.   *5 South Salina Street*

CITY.   *Syracuse, N. York*

NAME.   *Mr John Eilers*

STREET, NO.   *100 Fayette Street*

CITY.   *Utica, N. York*

Notes to Addresses

MOTHER DELPHINA. Gibson had some correspondence with her about expenses for the sisters who arrived in Honolulu on Nov. 17, 1886. Gibson to Mother Delphina, Aug. 27, 28, Sept. 1, 1886, Archives of the Franciscan Sisters, Syracuse, N.Y.

MISS TANNER. See diary entries of Feb. 12, Mar. 12, May 19, 1886; Mar. 16, 1887. London directories show a *Mrs. Mary Payne* at the 13 Oakley St. address. A Mrs. Caroline Emily *Maberly* appears in the court section of the 1886 London directory, but there is nothing to connect her with 13 Oakley St. Anthony J. Camp, Society of Genealogists, London, to Jacob Adler, May 9, 1970; C. Edwards, librarian for Chelsea, to Jacob Adler, Apr. 22, 1970.

RANDOLPH C. WANT. See diary entry of Jan. 16, 1886.

FATHER BONIFACE SCHAEFER. See diary entry of Nov. 17, 1886.

MRS. ELINOR GIBSON. Possibly Gibson's sister-in-law. At least two of his brothers had lived in the New York area.

WM. H. ROBB, G. H. MUNSON. Munson, a newspaperman, called at the offices of the *Advertiser* on Mar. 23, 1886. *Pacific Commercial Advertiser*, Mar. 24, 1886. Munson and Robb were among the founders of the Amsterdam, N.Y., board of trade. Robb was one of the founders of the hospital there and also a trustee of the library. Ethel Robb to Jacob Adler, Jan. 31, Feb. 12, 1970. One may speculate that through Munson's visit, Gibson entered into some correspondence with Dr. Robb. There is no evidence that Robb ever came to Hawaii.

MRS. LUCY T. MILLIE, possibly Gibson's sister.

JOSEPH E. GAUNDER. See diary entry of May 17, 1886, and corresponding note.

JOHN EILERS, father of *Sister M. Crescentia* Eilers. Letter, Sister M. Cleophas, Saint Clare Convent, Utica, N.Y., to Jacob Adler, Oct. 28, 1969.

1887

#2

Honolulu Apr 29th 1887.

Dear Mr. Gibson

When reports
first came to me of the denials you made regarding our
engagement I sought an interview with you and you de-
clared to me emphatically that
you had never denied it,
When you called upon me
Monday last your words so
reassured me, that I had perfect faith and confidence in
all you said. Pardon me if I
confess to you that my confidence
is a little shaken. Since I saw
you. I have heard so much, it
has come so direct, that it re-
quires an explanation. I cannot and will not be placed

in this equivocal position
You can never accuse me of
being unreasonable. I have
deferred to your wishes as much
as was consistent with what
was justice to me, and I have
not been selfish in this matter.
But now I think of myself—
for if what I hear is true, you
have given me no protection
at all, a strange manner for
a man to act towards a woman
when he has professed to love
and has promised to marry.
I still feel that when I see you
you can disabuse my mind
of any injustice done me through
you, therefore I shall restrain
my feelings and still trust
in you. There is only one
way to clear a mystery that
is by an explanation. Let

me see you as soon as possible
As you did and go to Waikiki
as you told me you intended
I presume you will not go
this week. until the weather
more
settled, Try and let me see
you this morning, You can
manage to snatch a few moments
from the office and I shall
be in a fever of impatience until
I do see you, I will remain
at home and expect you.
Hoping that you are well, and
that you will comply with my
request without delay, I remain
Yours affectionately
Flora

Delivered by Mr. Truvil.

Flora Howard St. Clair to Gibson, April 29, 1887. Evidence in
breach of promise suit. *Archives of Hawaii*

KAMEHAMEHA DAY!

THIRD ANNUAL
RACE MEETING!
---OF THE---
Hawaiian Jockey Club
---TO BE HELD---
AT KAPIOLANI PARK
---ON---
JUNE 11th AND 12th, 1886

FIRST DAY, JUNE 11, 1886.

1—HONOLULU PLATE.
RUNNING RACE—Half mile dash, open to all.

2—KAPIOLANI PARK PLATE.
RUNNING RACE—¾ Mile dash, open to all horses bredin the Kingdom that have never run at any meeting of this Association.

3—KING'S PLATE.
TROTTING & PACING RACE—Mile heats, best two in three; free for all horses not having a record of three minutes or better; to be owned and driven by members of the Jockey Club.

4—HAWAIIAN JOCKEY CLUB CUP.
RUNNING RACE—A sweepstake of $50 added; cup to be won by the same person twice, the second winning to be at any future Annual Meeting; one mile dash, open to all three-year-olds: sealed nominations, inclosing a fee of $10, to be sent to the Secretary of the Hawaiian Jockey Club on or before 2 p. m., on the 4th day of June. Final acceptances as to the balance of sweepstakes on or before 2 p. m., on the 10th of June. Second trial—Cup run for last year.

5—OCEANIC PLATE.
RUNNING RACE—One mile dash, free for all Hawaiian bred horses; maidens allowed 5 pounds.

6—WAIKAPU CUP.
RUNNING RACE—A sweepstake of $25 added, three-quarter mile dash, open to all two-year-old Hawaiian-bred horses. Cup to be won by horse beating the 2 year old record 1:23.

7—KAMEHAMEHA PLATE.
RUNNING RACE—One and one-half mile dash, open to all.

8—PONY RACE.
RUNNING RACE—Mile dash, open to all ponies of 14 hands or under.

SECOND DAY, JUNE 12, 1886.

1—GOVERNOR DOMINIS' PLATE.
RUNNING RACE—Three-quarter mile dash, free for all.

2—LUNAMAKAAINANA PLATE.
TROTTING RACE—Mile heats, best two in three; open to all Hawaiian-bred horses.

3—ROSITA CHALLENGE CUP.—$— ADDED.
RUNNING RACE—Mile dash, free for all; winner to beat the record of "Rosita," 1:47¾. Cup to be run for annually and to be held by the winner until his time is beaten at a regular meeting of the Association.

4—QUEEN'S PLATE.
RUNNING RACE—Mile dash, free for all Hawaiian-bred horses.

5—THE HAWAIIAN PLATE.
TROTTING PACING RACE—Mile heats, best two in three; All horses having a record of 2:30 or better to go to wagon.

6—HIS MAJESTY'S CUP.
RUNNING RACE—A sweepstake of $— added, one and a quarter mile dash; free for all three-year-olds, owned by members of the Club. The Cup to be run for annually.

C. O. BERGER,

Kam Day Race Ad

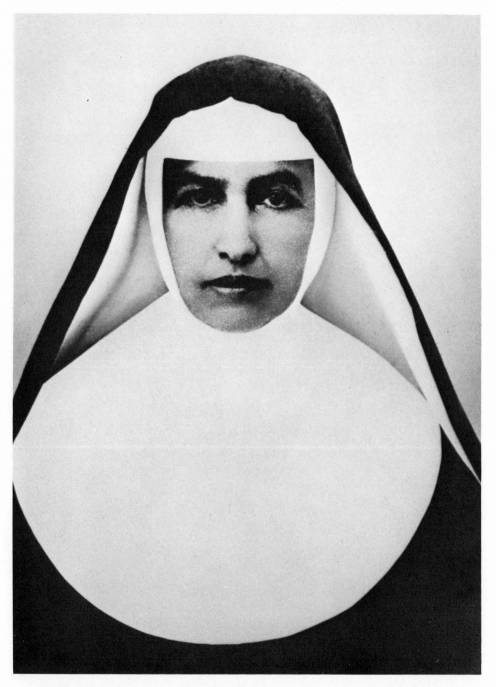

Mother Marianne (Barbara Kopp), 1836–1918. *Sisters of St. Francis, Syracuse, N.Y.*

Mother Marianne, *top center*. Others, *left to right:* Sister Crescentia, Sister Elizabeth, Sister Benedicta, Sister Leopoldina. *Sisters of St. Francis, Syracuse, N.Y.*

Gibson, Franciscan Sisters, and girls from Kapiolani Home, in front of home. *Archives of Hawaii*

Gibson's place card for King Kalakaua's fiftieth birthday dinner,
November 29, 1886, at Iolani Palace. *See* diary notes for this date.
Archives of Hawaii

SAT., JAN. 1 — *A beautiful day. Official calls on Mr Wodehouse, Mr Feer, Senhor Canavarro and Mr Ando.*

Called on the Walkers and Mrs Dudoit and Miss Corney — Mrs Howard.

I attended the luau at the Palace — tedious waiting from 2 till ½ past 3 P.M. — waiting for the King — did not appear — unwell, last night's debauch.

Called at the Convent at 5 P.M. A cordial sweet greeting from all the Sisters.

Bishop Hermann, Father Leonor and Father Clement called on me this forenoon. I spoke about a chapel — St Lucy.

Sent to Convent for the Sisters' dinner a roast turkey and 3 mince pies.

Pages containing the following dates have been cut out of the 1887 diary, under circumstances unknown to the editors: January 13–14, February 28–March 1, March 8–11, May 13–16, June 14–17, June 20–23, July 8–11, July 18–25. Except for these dates, it may be assumed that any dates missing in the text contain no entries.

JAN. 1. *Mrs. Anna Dudoit* ran a boarding house, Haleakala or Dudoit mansion, at Fort and King streets. She was the widow of Jules Dudoit, one-time French consul in Honolulu.

Miss S. F. Corney, principal of Pohukaina school for girls. *Daily Bulletin*, July 22, 1886.

Luau at the Palace, part of the celebration of Queen Kapiolani's birthday. Gibson offered a toast to the queen "which was responded to with three rousing cheers." The king was reported "unable to attend through indisposition." *Pacific Commercial Advertiser*, Jan. 3, 1887.

Proposed chapel to St. Lucy, doubtless in memory of his mother, Lucy Murray Gibson. Gibson's writings and writings about him reveal practically nothing about his mother. Nothing came of the chapel project.

SUN., JAN. 2 — *A beautiful day. Tone of health very good. Mrs Bickerton and Mrs Wood called.*

Dr Brodie called to speak of Sister Charles' state of health — must be well nourished with a little wine.

Drove to Convent this P.M. *and took a bot. of Port wine and a bot. of whiskey for Sister Charles. A few minutes with M.*

Spoke of my long cherished purpose to erect a chapel to be dedicated to St Lucy in memory of my Mother — and connect with it a small general hospital. I hope to live near M. and her Sisters, or have them live near me.

JAN. 2. *Mrs. M. A. Wood,* teacher at Pohukaina school for girls. *Hawaiian Gazette,* July 27, 1886.

MON., JAN. 3 — *Making some preparation at house for return of Talula and the children. Fixed up Talula's room. Mrs Bickerton called in to help about the arrangements. A large new Koa bedstead. Kahili brought a lot of large pulu ferns from the mountains.*

A happy hour at Kakaako.

M. and Sr Crescentia called on the Bishop. He spoke enthusiastically about my purpose to build a chapel and asylum to be dedicated to St Lucy, to which I referred when he called on me on New Year's Day. He evidently understands that the Sisters are to cooperate in the matter. That is my fondest hope — to cooperate with M.

JAN. 3. *Pulu.* "A soft, glossy, yellow wool on the base of tree-fern leaf stalks." It was used to stuff pillows and mattresses and was once a minor Hawaiian export to California. Pukui-Elbert, *Hawaiian Dictionary.*

TUES., JAN. 4 — *Stormy morning. Roused out of bed at ¼ to 6 this morning by telephone that the* W. G. Hall *was entering the harbor. Telephoned for carriage and I was at the wharf by 6 o'clock to meet Talula, Fred and the children. All well. Glad to see them.*

Spent a very pleasant hour with the King this forenoon. At Kakaako 4 P.M. *So happy with M. How noble and how good. How much I love her.*

Raining off and on all day.

Edith Turton came with the folks and [incomplete]

WED., JAN. 5 — *Raining all day — oppression of the weather. Troubled with cough. Have not had an attack for a long time. The children fatigue me — though happy to see them.*

A delightful hour with M. Took little Sister Mary Lucy with me to Kakaako — great entertainment to Sisters Irene and Cyrilla.

JAN. 5. *Little Sister Mary Lucy* is of course Gibson's granddaughter, Talula Lucy Gibson Hayselden.

THURS., JAN. 6 — *At Palace — the King urges that the Band be sent with the Queen to London.*

Called on Mrs Howard this forenoon.

Did not go to Kakaako.

Bad cough this morning. Continued rain — an extraordinary season of rain for the past five weeks.

FRI., JAN. 7 — *At Kakaako 10 A.M. M. an invalid with headache. Dr Brodie at Hospital to tap old Kaauwa. Rained all night — and showering during the day.*

JAN. 7. *Dr. Brodie taps old Kaauwa* [Kaaua]. "Taps" doubtless refers to bloodletting. The Rev. J. Kaaua was an inmate of the Branch Hospital. He conducted Protestant services there. *Report of Board of Health to Legislature of 1886*, p. 9.

SAT., JAN. 8 — *Light rains all day — off and on.*

Aholo agrees to provide Lahaina with hydrant water.

At Kakaako this P.M. M. the same tender friend as ever, who receives me affectionately — yet I need a companionship she cannot give me. But a strong and constant love binds me to her. What a pure, true and noble character.

SUN., JAN. 9 — *The weather oppresses me. A long talk with the King. Talked about the purchase or charter of the* Explorer.

A weary day at the house. Telephoned to M. —

disappointed. She may be weary and dull owing to the same causes.

MON., JAN. 10 — *Cabinet meeting at noon at the Palace. Discussion about the Br[itish] St[eame]r* Explorer, *and the Government printing. Kea at the house.*

A happy hour with M. Yesterday's dulness [sic] *completely cleared away. The sweetness and fondness of her manner completely satisfies my heart.*

JAN. 10. *Kea at the house.* John M. Kea, a clerk in the attorney general's office. At the cabinet meeting Gibson and Attorney General Antone Rosa had been appointed to explore ways of publishing "By Authority" notices. This resulted in the *Hawaii Government Gazette* (not to be confused with the Opposition party newspaper, the *Hawaiian Gazette*), published weekly for about five months beginning Feb. 7, 1887. Cabinet Council Minute Book, Jan. 10, 27, 1887.

TUES., JAN. 11 — *Passed a very bad night.*

WED., JAN. 12 — *Arrival of Steamer* Australia.

The King, commenting on letter of H. A. P. Carter who gave a credit about witholding [sic] *preliminary bond to Hoffnung which was due to me, as H. M. said, remarked on the subject — "The more I hear from that man (C) lately, the less I like him." If Bush does well on his present mission, he will succeed Carter.*

The two native Ministers not in sympathy with me — we will have to part.

At Kakaako this afternoon — a happy hour.

The Mother Superior Marianne called at the house on Talula today.

SAT., JAN. 15 — *Examined the* Explorer. *Propose to purchase her as a Government vessel to send to Samoa to carry Bush on his several missions.*

At Kakaako this afternoon.

SUN., JAN. 16 — *My Birthday — A sweet note from M. — so I called at the Convent and was made happy.*

Bishop Hermann and Father Leonor called on me.

A talk with the King about the Explorer. *He said that Aholo and Kanoa were opposed to the purchase of her. It is too much my enterprise. These natives are opposed. I am sorry to have our Polynesian movement checked.*

JAN. 16. *My birthday*, Gibson's sixty-third, according to the newspapers, but more likely his sixty-fifth. Princess Liliuokalani wrote in her diary: "...63 years old but he looks all of 78. Poor Gibson, why should they put all the blame on him only?" Queen Liliuokalani Diary, Jan. 16, 1887, Archives of Hawaii.

MON., JAN. 17 — *Celebration of my birthday. The Reformatory School band at the house 7.30 A.M. to serenade me. All the boys of the school came and sang.*

A dance in my hall this evening. A very stormy afternoon — strong wind with scads of rain, yet the people turned out well — over 250 persons present. The King in good spirits, and spent two hours with me.

The bad weather affects me painfully. My cough very bad.

JAN. 17. *Dance in my hall.* This was a spacious lanai next to Gibson's home. The Royal Hawaiian Band played, led by bandmaster Berger on first violin. "Mr. Gibson's portrait in crayons was suspended at one end of the room, which at the time it was executed a few years ago, was a life-like portrait, while his presence showed plainly the sear and yellow leaf, indicative of his fast approach to that . . . allotted time of man, three score years and ten. Still Mr. Gibson looked well last night, and though he did not join in the mazy waltz, he was active and ever attentive to his numerous and notable well-wishers." *Daily Bulletin,* Jan. 18, 1887.

TUES., JAN. 18 — *Had a good night's rest. Went to Kakaako at 10 A.M. in a joyous mood — but was not satisfied.*

Talked earnestly with the King about the purchase of the Explorer. *He is convinced and with me. Told me to call a Cabinet early in the morning.*

WED., JAN. 19 — *A Cabinet Council at the Palace 7 A.M. The King determined about purchase of* Explorer — *so decided in Council. I and Aholo a Committee to make purchase. We went at 8 A.M. to Hotel and found Mr Arundel. Concluded purchase for $20,000 in four instalments. I have carried my point, and the Polynesian movement will not be checked.*

An hour with M. — a pleasant hour — yet not satisfied.

JAN. 19. *John T. Arundel,* owner of the *Explorer,* was himself
an explorer and Fellow of the Royal Geographical Society.
He lectured in Honolulu on "Islands of the Pacific."
Hawaiian Gazette, Jan. 18, 1887; *Daily Bulletin,* Jan. 22, 1887.

THURS., JAN. 20 — *Arranging details about purchase of
the* Explorer.

*Spoke to the King about rumors in respect to his having
received a large sum from some Chinamen for granting
the opium license. Satisfied with the King's explanations
— but I think Junius Kaae took some money and so
compromised the King's name.*

With M. at Kakaako. She not very well.

JAN. 20. *Opium license.* Many items in the Honolulu newspapers
for January show that tongues of the residents were
wagging furiously about an opium scandal. A "By Authority"
notice of Dec. 31, 1886, by L. Aholo, minister of interior,
indicated that the license had been granted to Chun Lung
for four years from Jan. 1, 1887, under a law approved on
Oct. 15, 1886. *Pacific Commercial Advertiser,* Jan. 5, 1887.
A notice of Jan. 10 gave regulations for sale of opium under
the law. The licensee was to pay $30,000 a year in advance.
Pacific Commercial Advertiser, Jan. 12, 1887.

Junius Kaae had been appointed registrar of conveyances
on Oct. 30, 1886. All the newspapers decried the
appointment.

FRI., JAN. 21 — *Completed the purchase of the* Explorer *—
the vessel delivered to the Min. of Interior, Aholo. I
will now take charge of her as Secy. of Navy — an empty
title — but I will push this matter, our Polynesian
confederation. Hawaii has the elements and prospects of*

*a commanding Polynesian state — Kalakaua shall be a
King.*

*At Kakaako this forenoon. Did not intend to go today
— but* my little girl *said by telephone she wanted to
consult about certain repairs of Kalakaua [Kapiolani?]
home — and I was so happy to go — and be with
her. How I love the noble woman. I was so happy with
her.*

JAN. 21. *Explorer delivered to Aholo,* who was accompanied
by P. P. Kanoa, minister of finance. J. A. Hassinger, chief
clerk of the interior department, ran up the Hawaiian flag.
Pacific Commercial Advertiser, Jan. 22, 1887. Possibly a
bit of diplomacy by Gibson because Aholo and Kanoa had
opposed the purchase.

Secretary of Navy. Gibson became secretary of war and of
the navy Oct. 21, 1886. Royal Commissions, 1882–1887,
Archives of Hawaii.

Kalakaua [Kapiolani?] home. A Kalakaua boys home at
Kakaako was completed about Apr. 25. *Pacific Commercial
Advertiser,* May 2, 1887.

SAT., JAN. 22 — *Busy with instructions for Mr Bush.*

*At Convent this afternoon with baby Rachel. The good
Sisters delighted with the little pet. The little darling
shows a marked attachment for M.*

SUN., JAN. 23 — *M.'s birthday — wrote M. an earnest
loving note. She said in her reply my words brought tears
to her eyes. Sent a cherry pie to Convent.*

*Whilst I was at the Palace on Samoan affairs, Mr
Wodehouse called to say he had received an instruction*

from his Govt. — "to discourage the Haw. Govt. from interfering with the affairs of the Navigators' Islands." A check — but can be met. I have neglected Mr Wodehouse. Must correct this.

Put a thapsia plaster on my breast last night — a counter-irritant to cure my catarrh.

JAN. 23. *Wodehouse to discourage Hawaiian interference in Samoa.* Julian Pauncefote, undersecretary in the British Foreign Office, to Wodehouse, No. 23 confidential, Dec. 28, 1886. FO 58/219, British Public Records Office.

MON., JAN. 24 — *The transfer of the* Explorer *to Foreign Department. Mr Neumann said to me very warmly this morning that I had made a good move in placing the Reformatory School boys in this new training ship.*
With M. — warm and happy.

TUES., JAN. 25 — *The thapsia plaster stinging my back.*
Gov. Kanoa goes to Kauai and leaves me in charge of Finance Office.
With M. this afternoon — somewhat disappointed.

WED., JAN. 26 — *Gov. Kanoa went to Kauai and left me in charge of Finance Office as acting Min. of Finance.*
Did not call at Kakaako. M. in town — called at Board of Health office. Met Roche.

THURS., JAN. 27 — *Cabinet meeting —* Government Gazette — *expenses of* Explorer — *to be renamed*

Kaimiloa — *letter of Wodehouse about discouraging
H. M.['s] Govt. in respect to Samoa.*

*At Kakaako in the forenoon. M. in town. I drove into
town — and saw her vehicle at Dillingham's. She likes to
go shopping.*

*Went to Kakaako [in] afternoon, 4 P.M. M. made me
happy — a fond heart's expression.*

JAN. 27. *Explorer renamed Kaimiloa,* literally "the far
seeker," Hawaiian for *Explorer.*

Dillingham & Co., a general merchandise store on Fort
Street. One of the principal partners was Benjamin F.
Dillingham, well-known entrepreneur and railroader.

FRI., JAN. 28 — *A distracting attack of my cough this
morning. A thunder storm last night — heavy rain.*

Ordering repairs on the Kaimiloa.

*At Kakaako — a subdued expression seems to reject
the previous warmth. Cherries a cross — and a cause of
suffering — soreness — my heart down — may hope
for the kind affection of a daughter — but no ardor —
respect and affection for the Pres., Bd of H[ealth] —
and no more.*

*A pleasant hour with the King at noon. H. M. wants
to call an extra session of the Legislature.*

SAT., JAN. 29 — *A very bad attack this morning — a long
sleepless night. Can I not control this agitation of hopes
and fears? It overmasters me.*

Arranged for supplies and labor on the training ship.
At Kakaako — a happy hour with M.
Talula about to be confined.

SUN., JAN. 30 — *Much better today. Wrote a note to M.*
expressive of my good state of feeling. An affectionate
reply. Sent a little wine and ale to the Convent.

The great volcanic eruption affecting the weather —
a heavy, smoky atmosphere — heavy rainfalls — thunder
& lightning.

JAN. 30. *Volcanic activity* began about Jan. 15 on the south
slope of Mauna Loa on the island of Hawaii. An account
in the *Advertiser* of Jan. 26 mentions 618 earthquakes
and a lava flow one to three miles wide.

In the *Gazette* of Feb. 1, a comment on Honolulu
weather: "This disturbance of the elements is, no doubt,
due ... to the machinations of Madam Pele [the volcano
goddess]."

A writer in the *Bulletin* of Jan. 28 theorized "that the
immediate cause of Pele's present display of wrath ... was
solely ... due to the purchase of the Explorer ... when
there is a dearth of cash to meet necessities."

TUES., FEB. 1 — *The Princess Likelike said to be in danger*
— refuses food — affected by her native superstition
that her death is required by the spirit of Pele of the
Volcano.

The King is angry with his sister on account of her
obstinacy in refusing food.

FEB. 1. *Princess Miriam Likelike,* sister of King Kalakaua. She
was born in 1851. In 1870 she married Archibald Scott

Cleghorn, and they had one daughter, Princess Kaiulani, born 1875. Princess Likelike was governess of Hawaii, 1878–1880. She attended the Episcopal church, and was confirmed in 1882. *Hawaiian Gazette*, Feb. 8, 1887.

Her death required by Pele. This is of special interest because as a child Likelike had received a good deal of Christian religious instruction.

WED., FEB. 2 — *Death of Princess Likelike.*

THURS., FEB. 3 — *The Princess Likelike lying in state. I attended in full dress with decorations from 10 A.M. till 2 P.M.*

4 P.M. — went to Convent — saw M. a little while. Visited poor old Ka[a]uwa in company with her — the faithful sweet Sister of Charity. How proud I am to think I have a share in her affections — a place in her noble heart.

FRI., FEB. 4 — *Sent some fish with a note for M. to the Convent. No reply. M. sick — a bilious attack. Saw her for a few minutes in the parlor of the Convent at 4 P.M.*

Death of old Rev. Kaauwa at the Branch Hospital.

Meeting of the Privy Council — resolution of condolence to King & Royal Family.

FEB. 4. *Death of Kaauwa* [Kaaua]. Although he was Protestant minister at Kakaako, none of the English language newspapers published news or notice of his death. Oblivion was the lot of the leper.

SAT., FEB. 5 — *Much improved in health.*
Making progress in repairs of the Kaimiloa.
At Br. H. with M. this afternoon.

FEB. 5. *Repairs of Kaimiloa.* The *Gazette* estimated these
would cost $28,000. (In the end, they cost more.) The
editor also wrote that the country had as much need
for the ship "as a cow has for a diamond necklace."
Hawaiian Gazette, Feb. 8, 1887.

SUN., FEB. 6 — *Attended an Episcopal service at the Palace*
where the Princess is laid out in state this forenoon.
Bishop Willis officiated.

FEB. 6. *Alfred Willis* (1836–1920), Anglican bishop of
Honolulu, 1872–1902. Though Kalakaua had been confirmed
in the Anglican church at the time of his election in 1874,
he was not much of a churchgoer. Nevertheless Willis
was a staunch royalist, especially during the waning years
of the Hawaiian monarchy, 1887–1893. *The Episcopal
Church in Hawaii*, pp. 16–20. Fred and Talula Hayselden
were members of the Anglican church (St. Andrew's), and
Fred served as warden.

MON., FEB. 7 — *Return of my colleagues Kanoa and Rosa.*
Mail per J. D. Spreckels *from San Francisco — nine days'*
later news. Am. Senate ratifies new treaty on condition
of cession of Pearl Harbor.
At Kakaako — a happy hour with M.

FEB. 7. *Antone Rosa* (1855–1898), a part-Hawaiian who
became a great favorite of Kalakaua. Rosa was attorney
general, Nov. 15, 1886, to June 28, 1887. In mid-April 1887,
he was appointed vice chamberlain, assistant private
secretary to the king, commissioner of crown lands, acting
commander-in-chief of the armed forces, acting adjutant
general, and acting governor of Oahu! *Hawaii Government
Gazette*, Apr. 18, 1887. Obituary, *Pacific Commercial
Advertiser*, Sept. 10, 1898.

Cession of Pearl Harbor. A proposed supplementary
convention to the Hawaii-U.S. reciprocity treaty was
agreed to in the U.S. Senate on Jan. 20, 1887. The
supplement gave the United States the right to maintain
a coaling and repair station at Pearl Harbor. When
ratifications of the renewed treaty were exchanged in
November 1887, the Pearl Harbor amendment was
included. R. S. Kuykendall, *The Hawaiian Kingdom,
1874–1893*, pp. 392–393. *Daily Bulletin*, Feb. 9, 1887.

TUES., FEB. 8 — *The King is disposed to temporize on the
Pearl Harbor cession question. Says we must never consent
to the cession — but to appear to entertain the matter
for a while. Don't like any temporizing about this matter.
I will oppose the cession under all circumstances.*

*Called to see a Portuguese woman condemned by Dr
Brodie as a leper.*

*Did not go to Kakaako today. Painful to absent myself
one day.*

WED., FEB. 9 — *The King suggests a reciprocity treaty with
Canada for refined sugars.*

*I have an idea to propose to South Am. Pacific States,
to U.S. and to Japan — a conference in relation to
Polynesian affairs. Why should European bullies be
allowed to grab, and partition as they please, in Polynesia?*

A happy hour with M. this forenoon, 11 A.M. Talking about establishment of Sisters at Kalawao — ready — but "we will never be separated."

THURS., FEB. 10 — *Vandiver Brown at work making some ornamental figures with corals and sods in the grounds of my Queen St. house. There I hope to establish Mother Marianne and her Sisters in a Home of their own —*
With my little girl an hour this afternoon.

FRI., FEB. 11 — *Extravagance of the King in providing for the funeral — estimated to cost at least $23,000. No idea of value of money. Must do more for the substantial welfare of the People.*
A happy hour with my little girl — so faithful to her duty — so good — so pure. Visiting the sick in company with her. What a noble character. I reverence as well as love her.

SAT., FEB. 12 — *Anniversary of the accession and coronation. No celebration or reception — but I prepared an address on the part of Ministers, which Aholo read in the Hawaiian language and I read in English.*
At Kakaako this P.M. about half an hour — very happy with my little girl.
Arrival of Zealandia — despatches from Samoa. Bush doing well. Sent full particulars to Carter by mail today.
Sent letter and copy of Charter of Sisters to Rev Jos. M. Lesen at Syracuse.

FEB. 12. *Address for anniversary of accession* (1874) *and coronation* (1883) emphasized Kalakaua's policy of *Hooulu Lahui,* "increase of the nation," and his aim to "extend an enlightened sympathy to races which are like our own native Hawaiian endeavoring to attain to the blessings of self-government." "Address to the King by His Majesty's Ministers," *Hawaii Government Gazette,* Feb. 14, 1887.

Letter to the Rev. Jos. M. Lesen, provincial minister to the Franciscan sisters. The letter reads in part: "The King and Queen and all classes rejoice in the establishment of these ladies in the country as a blessing to the Hawaiian people. I am proud to have had a part in bringing them here, and I shall deem it one of the most important . . . duties of my life, and the most exalted of its pleasures, to continue to assist in the establishment and comfortable settlement of the Franciscan Sisterhood in the Kingdom." L. V. Jacks, *Mother Marianne of Molokai,* pp. 188–189.

MON., FEB. 14 — *Bishop Hermann called at Kakaako — he fears that certain English protestant Sisters will come to care for lepers at Molokai Settlement. So he wants Mother Marianne and her Sisters to go at once and occupy the field. This anxiety is owing to a letter received by Father Damien from Rev Mr Chapman of London who sent him a large sum of money contributed in London for our lepers.*

The Mother said to me today that she was ready and cheerful to go to Molokai. This expression annoyed me — that she was cheerful to go — but I suppose a mere expression of willingness.

FEB. 14. *London contributions for lepers,* reported to be about $5,000. See "English Sympathy with Father Damien," *Pacific Commercial Advertiser,* Apr. 11, 1887; also "The

Father Damien Fund," *Pacific Commercial Advertiser,*
Apr. 25, 1887. Both are highly critical of Father Damien
for giving the impression, in *The Times* (London, Mar.
12, 1887), that the lepers of Molokai were not being
properly cared for by the Hawaiian government. The
letter is quoted in full in *Pacific Commercial Advertiser,*
Apr. 25, 1887.

The Rev. Hugh B. Chapman was pastor of the Church of
St. Lukes (Anglican) in London. Steven Debroey, *Father
Damien* (London: Burns & Oates, 1966), p. 126.

Mother Marianne ready and cheerful to go to Molokai.
On Feb. 16 she wrote Father Lesen at Syracuse: "I
cannot begin to tell you all [Mr. Gibson] does for us,
if we were his own children he could not do more; to
have us firmly established here seems the one aim of his
life. . . .
  ". . . from the first it was expected that some of us
would sooner or later go to Molokai to care for the
suffering people there. . . .
  "And on the 9th of February His Lordship the good
Bishop [Hermann Koeckemann] called here . . . to ascertain
how we felt about going. . . . I told him how the Sisters
felt, that they, or rather we, were not only willing but
anxious, to go and care for the poor outcasts. He left with
a light heart, and has since then held council with Mr.
Gibson. . . . now arrangements are being made for four
Sisters to go to the leper settlement at Molokai. It may be
two or three months before things will be ready, as a
house will have to be built, and other arrangements
made for the Sisters' comfort before Mr. Gibson will allow
them to go. . . ." L. V. Jacks, *Mother Marianne of
Molokai,* pp. 62–63.

TUES., FEB. 15 — *Very much annoyed with Father Damien.
He has written abroad representing the lepers as neglected
by the Government, and has received about $6000 as
collections from charitable people. Bishop Hermann is very
much dissatisfied, and says Father D. has obtained money
on false pretenses — and now his Father D. disregards me
and the Board of Health, and undertakes to manage the*

leper settlement without consulting me in the least.
An hour with M. at Kakaako.

FEB. 15. *Lepers neglected by the government.* See letter
signed "A Patient at Kalawao" defending Father Damien's
use of the money received from England. The writer
said, for example, that the official clothing allowance of
$6.00 a year per person was not enough. *Pacific
Commercial Advertiser*, May 10, 1887.

WED., FEB. 16 — *Departure of* Australia. *Wrote fully to*
Mr Carter about Samoan affairs.

THURS., FEB. 17 — *Cabinet meeting — the conduct of*
Kapena — constantly drunk — proposed that he resign
the collector-generalship after the funeral of the Princess.
At Kakaako this morning — M. very lively. I went
again in the afternoon along with Lucy, Dada and Aupuni
to take some pictures to the Convent.

FEB. 17. *Conduct of Kapena.* The minutes of the meeting
refer only to "the alleged official unfitness of the Collector
General." Cabinet Council Minute Book, Feb. 17, 1887.

FRI., FEB. 18 — *The King urges me to demand Kapena's*
resignation — and agrees that Fred should take his place.
I hesitate — don't want to dismiss K. — a native and
noble warmly regarded by the people, and put my
son-in-law in his place.

*M. telephoned to me to come to her today. I went
enthusiastic and hopeful and came away disappointed.*

FEB. 18. *Don't want to dismiss Kapena.* He resigned as
collector general of customs on Apr. 30. On nomination of
Gibson, the privy council recommended A. S. Cleghorn,
widower of Princess Likelike, and he was appointed.
Pacific Commercial Advertiser, May 2, 1887.

SAT., FEB. 19 — *Arrival of Sr Renata at Kakaako.*

*Meeting of Board of Immigration. Continuation of
Jap[anese] immigration at my insistance.*

*At Kakaako. I lose hope of any close loving
companionship. Will be appreciated only as a useful old
friend.*

My breast hurting me badly.

FEB. 19. *Arrival of Sr. Renata,* from Kahului, Maui, doubtless
after a term of duty at Malulani Hospital, Wailuku.
Sister Renata Nash was one of the first group of
Franciscan sisters who came to Honolulu on Nov. 8, 1883.

SUN., FEB. 20 — *Walter's birthday.*

Breast and throat paining me very much.

*Talula is also suffering — probably a commencement
of her labor pains.*

*Went to Palace at 11 A.M. to attend religious service
by Bishop Willis. Suffered from cold drafts — much the
worse from going.*

FEB. 20. *Walter Hooulu Hayselden's birthday*, his eleventh.
He was Talula's oldest child.

MON., FEB. 21 — *Ordered a suit for Walter — the uniform
of the King's guard.*

*Still very unwell. Dr Trousseau with me, and forbade
my going out. I telephoned to Kakaako about being so
unwell. M. and Sr Renata called to see me about 5 P.M.
So happy to see the sweet kind face.*

TUES., FEB. 22 — *Feel a little better but the old complaint is
attacking me very severely.*

*Went to Palace at 10 A.M. To Kakaako at 11 A.M. —
the tender solicitude of the dear good women. M. my
"own precious child."*

Arrival of Gaelic. *Letters from Irwin — trouble about
Japanese deposits. I want to give them up to the Jap[anese]
authorities.*

FEB. 22. *Trouble about Japanese deposits.* A portion of the
wage earned by a Japanese contract laborer was withheld
by the planters according to an agreement between
Japan and Hawaii. The money was to be released to the
laborers on their return to Japan. The Japanese government
became concerned about the safety of these deposits and
transferred them from Hawaiian government control to
the Bank of Bishop & Co., Honolulu. *Hawaiian Gazette*,
Mar. 8, 1887.

WED., FEB. 23 — *Talula confined. A severe labor, so long protracted. A boy baby stillborn at about 10 P.M.*

I am very unwell — much cough — headache and nausea.

THURS., FEB. 24 — *Bishop read a funeral service over the remains of the dead baby.*

Talula doing very well.

At Kakaako — with M.

Continued cough — headache & nausea.

FEB. 24. *Bishop read funeral service.* The Right Reverend Bishop Alfred Willis of St. Andrew's Cathedral on Beretania Street.

FRI., FEB. 25 — *Talula getting better slowly.*

SUN., FEB. 27 — *Funeral of Princess Likelike.*

THURS., MARCH 3 — *The King mentioned to me to ask Kapena for his resignation. I advised to let him alone for a while. I don't want the odium of proposing his removal — and Kanoa afterwards put whom he likes in his place.*

Paid to Bishop Willis $1000 on acct of his school.

At Kakaako 4 P.M. — happy and dissatisfied.

MAR. 3. *Paid Bishop Willis $1,000.* This was part of a $20,000 appropriation for "repairs and permanent improvements to boarding schools." In the 1886 legislature Gibson had argued for support of private schools, especially for capital improvements. *Hawaiian Hansard*, pp. 463–464. Two such private schools, both Episcopal, were Iolani and St. Andrew's Priory.

SAT., MARCH 5 — *At Kakaako — happy and satisfied. My precious little girl.*

SUN., MARCH 6 — *Spent an hour at the Palace. The King is still determined upon the Queen's visit to Europe. I don't like it.*

Kanoa called to see me about the removal of Kapena. I said he was in his department, and he must ask his resignation.

MON., MARCH 7 — *At Kakaako, A.M. — a happy visit.*

SAT., MARCH 12 — *The anniversary of my union with M. — our first cherry.*

Went to Kakaako in the afternoon. Took a ring as memento of the day. Ruth 1 — 16, 17. W.♥M. March 12 — 1885. Fond commemoration of the day. So happy in this pure and exalted friendship.

MAR. 12. *Ruth 1:16,17.* "Entreat me not to leave thee, or to return from following after thee: for whither thou goest, I will go; and where thou lodgest, I will lodge: thy people shall be my people, and thy God my God. Where thou diest, will I die, and there will I be buried: the Lord do so to me, and more also, if aught but death part thee and me."

SUN., MARCH 13 — *Arrival of* Alameda — *news from Samoa* — *Act of Confederation. Will the great Powers let us confirm this act? If so, my scheme of Polynesian confederation will have fairly commenced.*

MAR. 13. *Arrival of Alameda.* Actually, she arrived the evening of the 11th and left the morning of the 12th for San Francisco. She had left Tutuila, Samoa, on Mar. 4. *Daily Bulletin,* Mar. 12, 1887.

Act of Confederation between Hawaii and Samoa had been amply heralded by rumors. The *Daily Bulletin* of Mar. 12 quoted a private letter from Samoa: "A Mr. Bush is making quite a stir here . . . with his proposition of alliance with the Honolulu government. He is a very poison to the Germans, who are anxious to annex Samoa."

MON., MARCH 14 — *Cabinet meeting in reference to Samoan affairs. Reading of papers* — *action deferred.*
    A happy hour at Kakaako.

TUES., MARCH 15 — *Preparing despatches for the* Australia *that leaves tomorrow.*
    Called on Mrs Howard — *not satisfactory.*
    Did not go to Kakaako today.

WED., MARCH 16 — *Departure of the* Australia. *Gave to Rossini $250* — *he leaves with me the marble bust of Victor Emmanuel as security.*
    Loaned to Vandiver Brown fifty dollars.
    Study of treaties of England, U. States, and Germany with Samoa. Unfair advantages taken by the strong and intelligent over the weak and ignorant.

A letter to Miss Tanner.

At Kakaako — very kind and nice — but my basket not full.

THURS., MARCH 17 — *Kamehameha [III] Day — St Patrick's Day — birthday of Maggie Walker. Bought a fan for Maggie — and sent with a note.*

Ordered a pound cake at Horn's — tastefully ornamented with "St Patrick," a † and "Sr R" in sugared letters on the icing. Sent as a compliment to Sr Rosalia — with a tender note to M. Messenger went at 3 P.M. — no answer — no return message not even by telephone. I was disappointed. About 9 P.M., M. telephoned to me about a supply of fish for the sick tomorrow. Was at prayers when my messenger came. Had not thought to send a message afterwards. More disappointed after the explanation.

Did not go to Kakaako.

MAR. 17. *Kamehameha [III, 1814?–1854] Day*, his birthday (there is some doubt about the date of birth), then a legal holiday but not today. Government offices were closed and a royal salute was fired. *Daily Bulletin*, Mar. 17, 1887.

Pound cake at Horn's. F. Horn modestly identified himself: "Practical Confectioner, Pastry-cook, Ornamentor and Proprietor of Honolulu Pioneer Steam Candy Factory, Bakery and Ice Cream Saloon." *Daily Bulletin*, Apr. 13, 1887.

SUN., MARCH 20 — *Arrival of Zealandia. Satisfactory news by mail.*

Cabinet meeting to consider Samoan affairs. Conditional ratification of confederation.

Carried letters this P.M. *to Convent. One from Rev J. Tuohy — name outside. Anxious to hear about him. M. did not wish to communicate particulars of his letter. Regret this. Had reason to believe that there was a peculiar interest between the two.*

MAR. 20. *Conditional ratification of confederation.* Essentially the confederation was ratified subject to Malietoa's treaty obligations to Germany, England, and the United States. Text of Malietoa's proclamation of Feb. 17, 1887, and Hawaii's ratification of Mar. 20 in *Hawaii Government Gazette*, Mar. 28, 1887. See also Cabinet Council Minute Book, Mar. 20, 1887.

MON., MARCH 21 — *A painful sore-throat.*

Bishop Hermann called — talk about Father Damien and Miss Flavien.

Went to Kakaako. M. a little restrained.

TUES., MARCH 22 — *At the Palace. The King very confidential — about Rosenberg's mesmerizings &c. Wants Neumann to have a job in connection with* Jap[anese] *immigration. I distrust N.*

At Kakaako. M. very quiet and reserved. The Tuohy letter has unsettled my mind somewhat. I wish it could be explained — I wish it was explained.

MAR. 22. *Rosenberg's mesmerizings.* Elias Abraham Rosenberg (1810–1887), of San Francisco, came to Honolulu in late 1886 or early 1887. He ingratiated himself with the king and became a kind of royal soothsayer. The king also gave him a job as appraiser of customs. Some time during his stay he gave the king a Jewish scroll of the law and a silver pointer for use in reading the scroll. The king gave Rosenberg a silver cup and gold medal. Rosenberg left Honolulu on June 7, 1887, and died in San Francisco on July 10. Jacob Adler, "Elias Abraham Rosenberg, King Kalakaua's Soothsayer," *Hawaiian Journal of History*, vol. 4, 1970, pp. 53–58.

WED., MARCH 23 — *Weary and depressed all day — yet busy at the Foreign Office.*

Did not go to Kakaako.

At the Palace today, in the course of conversation, the King said that should I die before him my body should be placed with Mr Wyllie's in the Mausoleum. In thinking over the inevitable event at times, my feeling has been that M. should have the disposal of my remains. I cherish that thought.

MAR. 23. *Robert Crichton Wyllie* (1798–1865), Hawaii's foreign minister from 1845 to 1865. His burial among the royalty of Hawaii partially indicates his importance. His biography remains to be written, doubtless delayed by his almost indecipherable handwriting.

Mausoleum. The Royal Mausoleum on Nuuanu Street, burial ground of the Kamehameha and Kalakaua dynasties. Gibson is not buried there.

THURS., MARCH 24 — *Arrival of the* Vitiaz. *Capt Makaroff called at 2 P.M. in full uniform.*

At Kakaako with some flowers, artificial and natural, to decorate the altar according to promise.

M. assisted me, genial as usual — and yet there is something. Happy when with her — but uncomfortable when I go away. The Tuohy letter sticks in my mind. I ought to ask her to explain all about it.

The King and Queen called at my house this ev. and spent an hour — very cordial.

MAR. 24. *Vitiaz*, Russian warship, bark-rigged; *Capt. S. Makaroff*, aide-de-camp to the czar. Among the complement of 344 men and officers were 3 Russian princes. *Daily Bulletin*, Mar. 24, 1887.

FRI., MARCH 25 — *Went at 9.30 A.M. to Convent with a choice pound cake for the Sisters — Feast of the Annunciation. Saw M. a few minutes — she seems as usual and yet I am unsettled.*

Called on S. W. Brown's wife.

Audience at Palace — Captain of Vitiaz and officers.

This evening attended drill &c of Honolulu Rifles. Presentation by the King of a flag. I prepared the speech for H. M. The King invited me to his side on the dais prepared for him — and Iaukea the Chamberlain gave way for me. How different with Judd — he stuck to the King's [side?] and I had to take a back seat.

MAR. 25. *Audience at the Palace.* Gibson presented J. F. Hackfeld, acting vice-consul for Russia, who then presented Capt. Makaroff and his officers, including the three Russian princes. The king's Household Troops formed a guard of honor. *Hawaiian Gazette*, Mar. 29, 1887.

Drill of the Honolulu Rifles. Gibson sat in the king's private box. In the speech written by Gibson, the king said: "The ladies — God bless them — though weak as warriors, are ever ready to inspire men to gallant deeds. . . . And now they give you this flag, which I am pleased to place in your hands . . . bear and defend it for the honor of Hawaii."

Capt. V. V. Ashford replied with a flowery speech ending: "We have the spirit of men who will stand by each other and by our duty in support of our country's flag . . . which we accept with gratitude, and with the promise that no conduct of ours shall sully it or the nation which it typifies." *Daily Bulletin,* Mar. 26, 1887. Fine words by a man who would soon be opposing the king in the revolution of June 1887.

Judd, probably Chief Justice Albert F. Judd, since he was one of the few persons who ranked near Gibson.

SAT., MARCH 26 — *Called on Mrs St Clair.*

> *At Kakaako this* P.M. *M. warm and nice and yet I feel a little unsettled.*

MON., MARCH 28 — *Very weak and languid — lost my appetite.*

> *At Kakaako this afternoon.*

WED., MARCH 30 — *Sick.*

> *At Kakaako.*

THURS., MARCH 31 — *At Kakaako.*

FRI., APRIL 1 — *A nice note from M. Took a fancy to have a little joke for the day. Sent the Sisters a cotton pie. Received a note of thanks before they had tried it.*

SAT., APRIL 2 — *At Kakaako.*

SUN., APRIL 3 — *Lost all relish for my early morning coffee — and no longer want any flavor of spirits prepared in any way.*

My stomach is sick.

MON., APRIL 4 — *At Kakaako. Tender nursing attentions of Sr Crescentia.*

TUES., APRIL 5 — *Mrs Walker called early to bring me some wine jelly and cakes. Very anxious about my rumored marriage — glad to know that it has no foundation, on my side.*

APR. 5. *Rumored marriage.* The columnist "Flaneur" had reported a rumor that Gibson "meditated taking unto himself a wife soon." *Hawaiian Gazette*, Mar. 29, 1887. In another column (Apr. 5) Flaneur reported "six to four on the widow!" (Flora Howard St. Clair).

WED., APRIL 6 — *At the Cathedral 7 A.M.*

Very languid and distressed with headache.

At Kakaako, and yet too much of invalid to have any enjoyment in the visit.

THURS., APRIL 7 — *Cabinet meeting — about loan matters, and special agent for Japanese immigration.*

Feel miserable — no appetite.

Mrs. St Clair called at the For. Office. Has been misrepresented.

138

Mrs Dudoit called at the house. Wanted a treat of gossip but got nothing.

At Kakaako. Happy with M.

APR. 7. *Mrs. Dudoit wanted a treat of gossip.* Mrs. Flora Howard St. Clair had stayed for a while at Mrs. Dudoit's boarding house.

FRI., APRIL 8 — *Very languid — no appetite.*

SAT., APRIL 9 — *Languid, nausea and no appetite. Ordered a lot of things for the dear Sisters at the Convent.*

At Kakaako this afternoon. Miserable in health yet comforted by my "little girl."

SUN., APRIL 10 — *Sent a large pound cake to the Convent this morning.*

At Kakaako this afternoon. Feeling very sick, and yet comforted in being with M.

MON., APRIL 11 — *Busy with preparations for the departure of the Queen and Princess Lydia.*

TUES., APRIL 12 — *Departure of the Queen per* Australia. *On board she whispered in my ear to write to her, and tell her all about home affairs. I had a long and pleasant talk with Comʳ Dickerson on board. He heartily endorses my general policy.*

139

<§1887§>

*A very annoying burning and drumming in my right
ear.*

At Kakaako — happy with M.

*Gave to Iaukea this morning a warm friendly letter
of goodbye with a neat gift — a handsome seal.*

APR. 12. *Departure of the Queen.* "Her Majesty the Queen,
accompanied by Her Royal Highness the Princess
Liliuokalani, take passage per Australia on the 12th inst.
to visit the United States . . . and Europe. The Royal Party
will proceed to Washington and call on the President . . .
and on arrival in London, Her Majesty will present the
congratulations of His Majesty and the Hawaiian People
to Her Majesty Queen Victoria on . . . the jubilee of Her
Britannic Majesty's accession to the Throne." *Hawaii
Government Gazette*, Apr. 11, 1887.

"Her Majesty Queen Kapiolani, accompanied by Her
Royal Highness Princess Liliuokalani; Lieutenant General
. . . John Owen Dominis; Major General . . . Curtis Piehu
Iaukea, His Majesty's Envoy Extraordinary and Minister
Plenipotentiary near the Court of St. James, and Colonel
James Harbottle Boyd, Secretary to the Minister, departed
by the Hawaiian Steamship Australia for the United
States . . . and Europe." *Hawaii Government Gazette*, Apr.
18, 1887. For a concise account of the trip, see R. S.
Kuykendall, *The Hawaiian Kingdom, 1874–1893*, pp.
341–343.

Commodore Dickerson of New York, a U.S. naval officer.
On Mar. 22 the king saw the commodore and his wife off to
the island of Hawaii. On Apr. 4 the Royal Hawaiian Band
gave a concert for him. Dickerson was also made a
member of the Royal Order of the Star of Oceania. *Pacific
Commercial Advertiser*, Mar. 23, Apr. 11, 18, 1887. Why
was all this attention paid to him? Possibly to gain U.S.
support for Hawaii's "Primacy of the Pacific" policy.

WED., APRIL 13 — *The burning and drumming in my right
ear — very troublesome.*

Dr Trousseau vaccinated the children.
He gave me a gargle and a tonic.
Did not go to Kakaako.

THURS., APRIL 14 — *Still the painful drumming in my ear.*
A Cabinet Council — about order of Govt. in case
of demise of Sovereign whilst heir apparent is abroad.
At Kakaako this afternoon. Tender attentions of Sr
Crescentia. M. syringed my ear with warm water &
borax — some relief. Happy in her affection.

APR. 14. *Order of Govt.* By resolution of the cabinet, Gibson
was requested to obtain the views of the supreme court
on the questions of order of precedence.

Heir apparent. Princess Liliuokalani, the king's sister.

SAT., APRIL 16 — *At Kakaako this forenoon. An hour with*
M.
  Arrival of Edith Turton from Lahaina.
  Went with all the family to the beach house in Kapiolani
Park. Staid there all night. Edith Turton went with us.

SUN., APRIL 17 — *An improved feeling, owing I judge to*
the beach atmosphere — so free from dust.

MON., APRIL 18 — *Came into town with Edith at 10 A.M.*
  At Kakaako for an hour this P.M.

TUES., APRIL 19 — *Torment of* that *woman. Impossible to*
recognize her in any way — a miserable intrusion.

A delightful hour at Kakaako. M. very warm and sympathetic.

APR. 19. *That woman.* Mrs. St. Clair, of course.

WED., APRIL 20 — *Delivered commissions of officers of* Kaimiloa *to the King.*

Went to Convent with the Japanese man Ganjiro [?] to point out to him the job of laying down tiles for side walk.

A pleasant half hour with M. and Sr Renata.

A letter from ------a miserable dose.

Party at the Palace — dance on account of Capt Wiseman & officers. I spent a couple of hours there.

APR. 20. *Letter from [Mrs. St. Clair].* The letter, dated Apr. 19, reads in part: "The unkind remarks that are being made when reports come that you deny our engagement, renders me almost distracted. . . . Please justify my confidence in you. At the same time relieve me from this most embarrassing position by at once openly acknowledging our engagement. . . . I will count the hours until I see you or hear from you." Law 2501, Archives of Hawaii.

Party at the Palace. The king handed out the commissions to Capt. Jackson and officers of the *Kaimiloa.* Their uniforms, fresh from the tailor shop, put the visitors, Capt. Sir William Wiseman and his officers, in the shade. The king proposed a toast to Capt. Wiseman and his ship, the *Caroline.* The captain responded not with a toast to Capt. Jackson and the *Kaimiloa* but "To the ladies, God bless them!" *Hawaiian Gazette,* Apr. 26, 1887.

THURS., APRIL 2 1 — *Alf Carter arrived at Branch Hospital from Leper Settlement. His family greatly excited about his coming here. Want him ordered back as soon as possible.*

At Kakaako this afternoon — talk with Carter.

A happy hour with M.

APR. 21. *Alfred W. Carter*, from leper settlement on Molokai. Later there was evidently a remission of his leprosy. On Mar. 29, 1890, while he was serving as a caretaker at the Kalihi (leper) Receiving Station, he committed suicide after the disease had been again confirmed. He left a wife and ten children. *Hawaiian Gazette*, Apr. 1, 1890.

FRI., APRIL 2 2 — *Mrs. H[oward] at For. Office. Promised to call upon her Monday next.*

The King went to Waimanalo.

SAT., APRIL 2 3 — *Sent carriage for M. and Sister Renata to visit the English Sisters.*

At Kakaako with M. this afternoon.

Talula and Fred attended this ev. tableaux &c at Musical Hall.

APR. 23. *Tableaux at Music Hall*. An amateur performance for the British Benevolent Society. "The programme comprised five *Tableaux Vivants*, followed by Bayle Bernard's screaming farce entitled 'On His Last Legs.' " *Daily Bulletin*, Apr. 29, 1887.

SUN., APRIL 24 — *Went with Talula, Fred and children to*
Kapiolani Park house — or the beach house as we call it.
 Adding to it new lanai, a broad veranda covered on the
sea side.
 Annoyed to learn that Mr Alfred Carter, condemned as
a leper, had returned from the Leper Settlement on
Molokai, and was at the Branch Hospital.

MON., APRIL 25 — *Called on Mrs Howard and Miss Waite.*
 At Kakaako this afternoon — very rainy. Saw Mr Alf^d
Carter — told him he must return to the Leper Settlement
— his friends did not want him here.
 With M. for an hour — somewhat restrained.

APR. 25. *At Kakaako this afternoon.* Gibson does not mention
that he showed an *Advertiser* reporter around the new
Kalakaua home for boys within the Branch Hospital
complex. *Pacific Commercial Advertiser*, May 2, 1887.

TUES., APRIL 26 — *Very rainy.*
 Did not go to Kakaako.

WED., APRIL 27 — *Very rainy.*
 Did not go to Kakaako.

THURS., APRIL 28 — *Continued rainy weather.*
 Health continues good.
 At Kakaako. Happy assurances of a noble friendship.
 Mr Alf. Carter returned to Molokai Leper Settlement
per Mokolii.

Search of For. Off. records — *important evidences in respect to British treaty.*

APR. 28. *British treaty.* See also 1887 diary entries for Apr. 29 and May 4. Gibson had instructed Iaukea, as diplomatic member of Queen Kapiolani's entourage, to seek revisions of Hawaii's treaty with Great Britain. Nothing came of this. R. S. Kuykendall, *The Hawaiian Kingdom, 1874–1893,* p. 341.

FRI., APRIL 29 — *The King returned late yest. ev. from Waimanalo. Saw H. M. this morning — in good spirits. Referred to opium money — said Kaae had it in his possession, with letters from T. Aki making it an absolute gift to H. M.*

> *Cabinet meeting at 1 P.M.*
> *Allowed $5,000 for the* Kaimiloa. *Br. treaty.*
> *Letter from Mrs H. — a miserable schemer.*
> *Did not go out this afternoon.*

APR. 29. *Opium money.* Tong Aki was to receive the license (authorized by the legislature of 1886) for a "gift" of $75,000 to the king. He actually paid, through Junius Kaae, $71,000. But Chun Lung made a larger "gift," $80,000, and the license went to him. In the revolution of 1887, one of the demands on the king was that he repay Aki. Repayment was not made because the king was heavily in debt. R. S. Kuykendall, *The Hawaiian Kingdom, 1874–1893,* pp. 353–354, 360, 405–406. Gavan Daws, *Shoal of Time* (New York: Macmillan, 1968), pp. 245, 247, 253. See also report in *Hawaiian Gazette,* May 17, 1887, based on some sixty pages of affidavits.

Letter from Mrs. St. Clair. The letter, dated Apr. 29, reads in part as follows: "When reports first came to me

of the denials you made regarding our engagement I
sought an interview with you. . . . When you called upon
me Monday last [April 25] your words so reassured me
that I had perfect faith and confidence in all you said.
Pardon me if I confess to you that my confidence is a
little shaken. . . . There is only one way to clear a mystery,
that is by an explanation." Law 2501, Archives of Hawaii.

SAT., APRIL 30 — *A happy hour at Kakaako.*
*Went with all the family to the Park house. Chinese
carpenters at work making additions.*

SUN., MAY 1 — *Feel much better at the house on the beach.*

MON., MAY 2 — *Came in to town this morning — and
returned to the beach house in the afternoon.*
An hour at Kakaako.

TUES., MAY 3 — *Arrival of the* Australia.
Did not go to Kakaako.

WED., MAY 4 — *Drove in to town about 9 A.M. Fred
remained with Talula, Aupuni and Rachel at the Park
house.*
Enna came in with us and the children going to school.
*Fred, Talula and babies returned to town unexpectedly.
Aupuni taken very sick, and Fred had a bad fall.*
*Trouble with Mr Wodehouse, on account of my
neglect of a notice to him of Iaukea's mission. He declines
to communicate through me to the King — applied to
Vice Chamberlain Rosa. Mr W. informed that he must
communicate through me.*
A happy hour at Kakaako.

MAY 4. *Iaukea's mission.* As envoy extraordinary and minister plenipotentiary, Iaukea carried Kalakaua's letter of congratulations to Queen Victoria on her jubilee. Iaukea was also to take up British policy in Polynesia and possible revision of Hawaii's treaty with Great Britain. R. S. Kuykendall, *The Hawaiian Kingdom, 1874–1893,* p. 341.

THURS., MAY 5 — *Anxiety about attitude of Wodehouse. Resolved to call on him personally. A satisfactory interview, and harmony restored.*

The King received Mr Wodehouse at noon. I was present. Mr W. informed me that the Govₜₖ of England & Germany would not consent to allow Hawaii to take part in a conference at Washington about Samoan affairs.

A letter from that intriguing woman Mrs H. A cause of much anxiety and worry.

Went to Kakaako at 3½ P.M. Calm and rest there.

MAY 5. *The King received Mr. Wodehouse.* The formal notice of the audience makes no mention of the Washington Conference, but quotes a letter of Mar. 28, 1887, from Queen Victoria to King Kalakaua. The letter, presented by Wodehouse, offered condolences on the death of Princess Likelike. *Hawaii Government Gazette,* May 9, 1887.

The United States, Great Britain, and Germany held a conference on Samoan affairs at Washington, D.C., in June and July. Hawaii was in fact excluded. Germany, with the consent of England, was trying to get control of Samoa. The United States opposed this, and the conference adjourned without agreement. R. S. Kuykendall, *The Hawaiian Kingdom, 1874–1893,* p. 337.

Letter from Mrs. St. Clair, dated May 5: "Your silence and indifference already too long continued, can be endured by me no longer.... unless you renew your visits to me, and freely admit our engagement no later (Monday, May 9th) I shall as (I must) conclude that you are insincere in your professions and promises. I shall take advice as to what actions may be necessary for my protection." Law 2501, Archives of Hawaii.

FRI., MAY 6 — *Anxious about the* Kaimiloa, *to get her off to sea.*

Called with Mr Willing the nurseryman at Kakaako. Only a few moments with M. to give her some instruction about her nursery.

Blowing and raining. Caught fresh cold, I am afraid, on the wharf looking after the Kaimiloa.

Trouble with my eyes.

Mr Webb my Secy. had a fall on the wharf and dislocated his right arm at the elbow.

MAY 6. *Carl Willing*, in charge of the government nursery on Beretania Street. *Daily Bulletin*, June 2, Nov. 5, 1887.

Gibson's eye trouble and Webb's fall. These were the first of many signs that the gods were not smiling on the *Kaimiloa*. Joseph S. Webb, secretary of the foreign office, had been commissioned paymaster of the navy on Apr. 21. *Hawaii Government Gazette*, May 2, 1887.

SAT., MAY 7 — *An inflamed left eye — very bad all day. Dr Trousseau calls it conjunctivitis — eased pain with cocoaine* [sic]. *Eye troubling me very much all day.*

Dictated a good deal of correspondence for Carter in Washington and Iaukea in London.

Remained in my room all day. A trying time — I am almost blind — and my secretary disabled in his writing arm.

SUN., MAY 8 — *My eye continues very sore. Dr T. continues his treatment.*

In my room all day. Dictating letters to go by mail tomorrow.

MON., MAY 9 — *The eye a little easier but still painful. Procured smoked glasses.*

In my room all day. Busy dictating correspondence to go per Australia *which sailed at noon.*

Hoped to have heard from or seen M. today — disappointed.

Uneasy on account of schemes of that miserable widow which I hear of today. She is consulting the Ashfords.

Told Fred to mention casually to V. Ashford that I wanted to consult him about Canadian affairs.

TUES., MAY 10 — *Fred saw Clarence Ashford — much pleased about my wish in respect to Can[a]dian affairs. The widow was with Ashford when Fred called.*

At Kakaako. M. and Sisters Crescentia and Leopoldina expressed their sympathy and affection on account of my recent affliction.

Capt Jackson and his wife at the house. Want to coax me to help provide for a farewell entertainment. I objected.

MAY 10. *Farewell entertainment for Kaimiloa.* Capt. Jackson gave a farewell party at his Palama home on May 12. Gibson did not attend. *Hawaiian Gazette,* May 17, 1887.

WED., MAY 11 — *Proposed to the King that we send Kaimiloa direct to Samoa — and go to take possession of Necker and other small islands by and by. Agreed to — also that I send Webb to Samoa if he can go. Agreed that Gulick be offered the tax collectorship for Hono* [*lulu?*]. *I proposed him some time ago. H. M. wants me to help Frank Godfrey.*

At Kakaako 3 [*?*] *P.M. The band there. Happy with M. Home sweet home.*

MAY 11. *Webb to Samoa.* He was to act as adviser to John E. Bush at Apia, Samoa. He was also to act as chargé d'affaires at such times as Bush might be away from Apia. Gibson to Bush, May 14, 1887, Letterbook, Consular and Miscellaneous, 1873–1900, p. 162, Archives of Hawaii. Beyond question Webb's main job was to keep Gibson informed of what was going on in Samoa.

TUES., MAY 17 — *Anxiety about the* Kaimiloa. *Waked up last night at midnight — report of riot on board. Thiron and McDonald to be dismissed — also Kaluahine.*

Bad wet weather.

Ordered the Kaimiloa *to go to sea at 5 P.M. More trouble — the King ordered sailing to be postponed till tomorrow morning.*

Talula, Fred and three small children went to beach house. Walter and Lucy remained with me.

MAY 17. *Riot on Kaimiloa.* A "general state of insobriety and insubordination" resulted from too much gin. Captain Jackson and Gibson had to go aboard to put down the disturbance. *Daily Bulletin,* May 17, 1887. See also "The Kaimiloa — Disgraceful Conduct and Dismissal of Officers," *Pacific Commercial Advertiser,* May 18, 1887; also in same issue, editorial "A National Disgrace" — "the public scandal becomes intolerable when officers holding the King's commission set an example of insubordination and misconduct to the men subversive of all discipline."

On Apr. 21 *Henry L. Thiron* had been commissioned chief engineer; *David McDonald,* sub-lieutenant; and *James Kaluahine,* acting sub-lieutenant. So their terms as officers in the king's navy lasted less than a month.

WED., MAY 18 — *Departure of the* Kaimiloa *this morning. Relief.*

Fred and Talula returned from the beach.

At Kakaako — a happy hour.

Engaged Frank Godfrey.

MAY 18. *Departure of Kaimiloa.* In "Gone at Last," the *Daily Bulletin,* May 18, commented: "There is ground to fear that riot will run high ere she returns to these shores."

Engaged Frank Godfrey, possibly as an informer against the Honolulu Rifles and the Hawaiian League and their intrigues against the government. Godfrey, a copyist and clerk, was appointed ordnance sergeant in the Rifles in early April. *Hawaiian Gazette,* Apr. 12, 1887. See also 1887 diary entries of May 11 and 27.

THURS., MAY 19 — *Movement of that devilish woman — getting up a breach of promise case. Enna's report.*

At Kakaako.

SAT., MAY 21 — *Served with a summons — breach of promise suit.*

At Kakaako.

Went to beach house.

MAY 21. *Breach of promise suit.* On May 17 the *Gazette* columnist Flaneur reported that "Holy Moses" (Elias Abraham Rosenberg, the king's soothsayer) had cast a horoscope for Gibson in which a suit for damages appeared. The suit, filed on May 21, asked damages of $25,000. *Daily Bulletin,* May 21, 1887.

SUN., MAY 22 — *Spent the day at the beach or Park house.*

MON., MAY 23 — *Returned to town this morning.*

Cabinet Council at noon.

Mr Rosa said to me — "The King is more attached to you than ever — since this blackmail breach of promise suit."

At Kakaako. M. knows all about suit. I think a little more earnest and affectionate.

TUES., MAY 24 — *Mr Smith, book[k]eeper of Haw[aiian] Carriage Man[ufacturin]g Co., called to speak of letter speaking about Mrs H. and her sister.*

Mr Hart called with Mr Cox. The latter proposes to have the suit discontinued for a consideration. I declined.

MAY 24. *Smith,* John F.

H. J. Hart, owner of the Elite Ice Cream Saloon, and possibly *Charles Cox,* a tailor. Later, in the St. Clair-Gibson breach

of promise case, Hart testified that one evening in May
Mrs. St. Clair and a gentleman whom Mr. Hart believed to
be Mr. Cox came in to have some ice cream. After they
had gone, the gentleman came back alone to buy some
cigars. Hart also testified that he had hoped to get a large
ice cream order for the wedding. *Pacific Commercial
Advertiser*, Oct. 31, 1887.

WED., MAY 25 — *At Kakaako. Rather sad — but I am
satisfied with the fine expression of affection.*

THURS., MAY 26 — *Did not go to Kakaako.*

FRI., MAY 27 — *The King urgent about purchase of
newspaper. I sent for Mr Wm. G. Irwin — agreed to
purchase* P. C. Advertiser *interest for $20,000 on behalf
of Gove[rn]m[en]t.*

*Paid down $2000 earnest money. The king had agreed
to advance $2500, half of first cash payment.*

*Sent Fred to get the money at the Palace. The King
not ready — wants to* borrow *the money. Would see me
later.*

Frank Godfrey wants to furnish information.
Did not go to Kakaako.

MAY 27. *King urgent about purchase of newspaper.* The
cabinet council had discussed the need to have a semiofficial
newspaper organ, presumably something more than the
Hawaii Government Gazette which devoted itself mostly
to formal announcements. The king appointed Gibson
and Attorney General Antone Rosa to look into the matter.
Cabinet Council Minute Book, May 21, 1887.

SAT., MAY 28 — *Cabinet meeting — commission to Canada — patrol of city — purchase of newspaper.*

The King was to take part in purchase of paper, but now wants to induce certain Chinese adherents to take stock — Chung Lung &c.

A note with some Japanese articles, tray and dishes, to M. at Kakaako. A sweet reply.

The King said this ev. that Chung Lung had backed out of newspaper investment because he had been charged $10 for a passport at Foreign Office.

MAY 28. *Cabinet meeting.* The Cabinet Council Minute Book does not show any meeting on this date.

Chung Lung charged $10 for passport. This is presumably the same Chung (or Chun) Lung who paid some $80,000 for the opium license. Landing charges for Chinese were increased from $2 to $10 on Feb. 1. Chung Lung had made a trip to San Francisco, and returned to Honolulu on Feb. 24. He doubtless had to pay the $10 fee. Apparently as a result of his complaint, the fee was reduced to $2.00. Cabinet Council Minute Book, June 2, 1887.

SUN., MAY 29 — *I sent for Chung Lung and explained to his satisfaction about passports. I also satisfied C. Alee, the Chinese Com. Agent.*

MAY 29. *C. Alee* (or Ah Lee), *Chinese commercial agent.* He had consular rather than ministerial or ambassadorial rank. Among other duties, he dealt with Chinese immigration to Hawaii.

MON., MAY 30 — *Chung Lung advanced $3000 toward purchase of paper.*

Talula and Fanny Bickerton paid a visit to the Sisters at Kakaako.

TUES., MAY 31 — *Mr Hayselden effected the purchase of all of Wm. G. Irwin & Co.'s interest in the P.C. Advertiser. Purchase of 240 shares of stock, $7200. Pay debt $13000 in two notes, $6500 each, 6 mos. and 1 year — signed by A. Rosa, H. M. Vice Chamberlain, and myself. I advanced $2800 of the purchase money.*

At Kakaako — spent a pleasant hour.

MAY 31. *Purchase of Advertiser.* "At a meeting of the stockholders held Tuesday afternoon [May 31] a portion of the stock changed hands, thus involving the necessity for a change in its management and a modification in the expression of its views on public matters. . . .

"With this issue the *Advertiser* takes a new departure, and its best efforts . . . will be directed towards expressing faithfully and fairly the opinions of His Majesty's Government." *Pacific Commercial Advertiser*, June 2, 1887.

"The Government resumes control of the paper [*Advertiser*] and it will henceforward be published as a Government organ." *Daily Bulletin*, June 2, 1887.

WED., JUNE 1 — *I have engaged Mr Horace Wright to assist me in preparing editorials for the P. C. Advertiser.*

Paid $1000 to Bishop Willis on account of his new school house.

THURS., JUNE 2 — *At Kakaako. Met there Bishop and Miss Willis.*

SAT., JUNE 4 — *Very weak and uncomfortable. A troublesome diarrhoea. Could not attend the King's luau to entertain the visiting Masons at Waikiki.*

Drove to Kakaako. A short while with M. Her tender sympathy for the invalid.

The Earl and Countess of Aberdeen, passengers per Alameda, *received by His Majesty.*

Mr Neumann forwarded to detective in San Fran. particulars about Mrs H. St. C.

JUNE 4. *Luau for visiting Masons,* one of many events honoring Edmund C. Atkinson, grand master of California Masons, and his party. (Kalakaua was himself a Mason.) Atkinson called the luau "a bountiful feast, strange and wonderful." He said he had been told he would find luau food unpalatable, but he had tried everything. In an undertone the king asked if he had eaten of the roast dog. Atkinson said he had done so — with much relish. *Pacific Commercial Advertiser,* June 6, 1887; *Daily Bulletin,* June 6, 1887.

Seventh Earl of Aberdeen (John Campbell Gordon, 1847–1934), lord-lieutenant of Ireland, 1886; governor general of Canada, 1893–1898. *Concise Dictionary of National Biography, 1901–1950.* He and the countess had been visiting in Australia and New Zealand.

SUN., JUNE 5 — *Spoke to the King about bad report from Samoa against Bush. H. M. proposed to send Mahelona to supersede Bush.*

JUNE 5. *Samuel W. Mahelona,* a native Hawaiian lawyer, had been a member of the legislature in 1866, 1867, 1868, and 1876. Index of Officeholders, Archives of Hawaii.

MON., JUNE 6 — *I advised the King against the sending of Mahelona — not qualified. H. M. agreed to the appointment of H. F. Poor as Chargé d' Affaires in Samoa. At Kakaako this afternoon.*

JUNE 6. *H. F. Poor as chargé d'affaires in Samoa.* Poor had gone to Samoa in December 1886 as secretary of legation.

WED., JUNE 8 — *At Kakaako about an hour this* P.M.

THURS., JUNE 9 — *Mr Sewall, U.S. Consul General for Samoa, took lunch with me. Came in the evening again with Sen[ato]r Whitney, Miss Whitney and Miss Tucker. Minister Merrill and Mrs Merrill with us. Some minstrel music — cakes & cream.*

Very much pleased with Mr Sewall — high hopes of his sympathetic cooperation with our legation in Samoa on Samoan affairs under a Hawaiian influence.

JUNE 9. *Harold M. Sewall* was on his way to Apia, Samoa, to replace the discredited Berthold Greenebaum. Sewall later wrote of his stopover in Honolulu: "[The King and Gibson], but especially the Minister dwelt upon the fact that the proposed relations of Hawaii with the South Sea groups were of a mild and benevolent nature, that Hawaii had had a similar mission to these Islands before, and that as regards Samoa, years ago missionaries of the Mormon Church had gone from here to proselyte there." H. M. Sewall, "Partition of Samoa" in *7th Annual Report of the Hawaiian Historical Society* (Honolulu, 1900), p. 12. In his Mormon days [1860–1864] Gibson had been in touch with the missionaries to Samoa.) On Aug. 12, 1898, Sewall as U.S. minister to Hawaii accepted from S. B. Dole sovereignty over the Hawaiian Islands in the annexation ceremony in front of Iolani Palace.

Sewall came in the evening again. Brief account of the party with guest list in *Daily Bulletin*, June 10, 1887.

California State Senator *George E. Whitney*, his daughter *Violet Whitney*, and Miss *Emma Tucker*, all of Oakland, Calif., were on the tour with the visiting Masons. On June 13 they had breakfast with the king at Iolani Palace. *Hawaii Government Gazette*, June 20, 1887.

FRI., JUNE 10 — *Good news per* Zealandia *about our Queen in England, and Samoan affairs. We have got our foot in Samoa, and it will not be taken away. I assured the King this morning of our hopeful prospects.*

At Kakaako a short while.

Talula, Fred and children went to Park [house] today — intending to stay all night — but returned in the evening.

Goodbye to Mr Sewall who left per Zealandia *for Apia.*

By instructions of the King ordered the recall of Bush — and the return of the Kaimiloa. *Poor [appointed] Chargé d'Affaires.*

SAT., JUNE 11 — *Kamehameha Day. Talula, Fred & children and Mrs Turton & Edith started at 8 A.M. for the Park, to be early at the races. Will stay at the beach house tonight.*

At 1 P.M. I went to Kakaako. Had a nice lunch at the Convent — some hot coffee & milk, boiled eggs and cherries. Came away at 4 P.M. M. a true daughter. Gave to lepers $10. Aupuni's birthday — gave him $5-pc. gold.

SUN., JUNE 26 — *Increasing rumors about public discontent, and that there is an armed league in opposition to the Government.*

MON., JUNE 27 — *Assurances of a widespread and dangerous organization — to subvert the Government.*
   Aholo and Kanoa resigned this afternoon without consulting me.

JUNE 27. *Widespread and dangerous organization.* The Hawaiian League, a secret, practically all-white organization, had been formed about the beginning of 1887. One of the leaders was Lorrin A. Thurston. It was composed mostly of persons who feared rising Hawaiian nationalism. One faction of the league wanted to reform the monarchy to take away power from Kalakaua. Another faction wanted annexation to the United States. The Hawaiian Rifles, a private military company which also got government support and recognition, became a secret military arm of the League. R. S. Kuykendall, *The Hawaiian Kingdom, 1874–1893*, pp. 347–352.

TUES., JUNE 28 — *Meeting of Ministers at 10 A.M. Resigned our offices. Hope that our resignations will quiet the public feeling.*
   At the Convent a few minutes.

WED., JUNE 29 — *A somewhat easier feeling since announcement of resignation of Ministers. The King now alarmed — will accept the extreme radicals.*
   Probable Ministry — W. L. Green, Godfrey Brown, J. O. Carter and Sanford B. Dole.

At Convent a few minutes to relieve alarm in respect to the state of the community.

Gave bond &c.

JUNE 29. *Probable ministry. William L. Green,* who had been minister of foreign affairs, 1874–1876, became minister of finance and was regarded as the head of the cabinet. He was probably the most conservative member.

Godfrey Brown, a member of the 1884 legislature, became minister of foreign affairs.

The other two appointments were much more radical than Gibson expected. Lorrin A. Thurston became minister of interior and Clarence W. Ashford attorney general. Thurston was one of Gibson's bitterest foes, and Ashford was the brother of Volney V. Ashford who was all for hanging Gibson. Godfrey Brown "represented the conservative wing of the reform movement and soon found himself out of sympathy with some of the policies and attitudes" of Thurston and Ashford. R. S. Kuykendall, *The Hawaiian Kingdom, 1874–1893,* pp. 402–403.

Sanford B. Dole and *J. O. Carter* did not become members of the cabinet at this time. Dole, one of the most prominent Opposition party members of the 1886 legislature, was active in the revolutions of 1887 and 1893; president of the Republic of Hawaii, 1894–1898; and first governor of the Territory of Hawaii. Carter was a member of the 1872 legislature, an officer of the prominent sugar and mercantile firm of C. Brewer & Co., and a member of Queen Liliuokalani's privy council from 1891 to 1893.

Gave bond &c. Presumably that he would not try to seize power again or try to repress the revolutionists.

THURS., JUNE 30 — *Threats of violence. My appeal to Preston, Bickerton and the King. Fred & family went to the Park house.*

Went to Convent to get vouchers signed. Bid goodbye — M.

The rifles at the Govt. building. I address a note to Lieut Col Ashford, asking protection of rifles. He ordered a detachment under Capt Fisher to guard my residence. I go to Govt. building to be protected there. Removal of guard — return to my house. Rumors of armed mob, purpose to lynch me. Col Ashford informs me that I will be shot down if I attempt to leave my house. The mob around my house — an anxious night. Faithful guard of Dan Lyons.

JUNE 30. *Threats of violence.* On the revolution of 1887, see R. S. Kuykendall, *The Hawaiian Kingdom, 1874–1893,* pp. 344–372, "End of the Gibson Regime."

A deadly serious letter in the *Hawaiian Gazette* of May 31 unwittingly burlesques the attitude of the revolutionists: "Men who lived here from the time of the Kamehamehas have seen a constitutional government changed into an absolute despotism and military rule.

"Some of the descendants of the men who forced King John to give the English people the Magna Charta are here.

"The descendants of those who fought on Bunker Hill are with us, and also Germans, who love liberty and right.

"Let us then act *unitedly, firmly, judiciously,* and the right will prevail, and we shall have the approval of the civilized world.

> "And right is right, since God is God,
> And right the day must win.
> To doubt would be disloyalty
> To falter would be sin."

Went to Convent. Sister Leopoldina has given an account of this last visit (*minor changes have been made in spelling and punctuation*):

"One morning when the doorbell rang, I was surprised that it should be Mr. Gibson. . . . I can ever see him as he was standing there, his bowed white head, drooping shoulders and snow white beard. When he came in he said in usual kind manner, 'I have come to say goodbye.'

" 'Are you going away?'

" 'No,' he said, 'my enemies are about to carry out their

threats of the last three years . . . they tell me this is my
last day. . . . Many times they have ordered me to resign.
The King and Queen are with me, they will not let me
resign. I do not mind much, only it was my great desire
to see the Sisters well established in the islands.'

"His gray head dropped . . . his thin old hands clasped
as in prayer. I hurried away to call Mother and the Sisters.
In a few minutes we were all gathered around him. We
were grieved, he had been so kind and fatherly to us.
His words were not many, but very kind. 'You need not
fear,' he said, 'they will not harm you, it is only me they
are after.'

"After saying goodbye he left us, and that was the last
time he came to see us." Journal of Sister Leopoldina
Burns, chap. 10, pp. 8–11. Archives of Franciscan Sisters,
Syracuse, N.Y.

Government building, or *Aliiolani Hale*, the present
Judiciary Building. It then contained the legislative hall
and government offices, including Gibson's. It is across
from Iolani Palace, to the south.

Capt. J. H. Fisher had taken command of Company C
of the Honolulu Rifles about May 30. *Hawaiian Gazette*,
May 31, 1887.

Daniel Lyons (d. July 14, 1895, at about fifty-five years).
A journalist who came to Hawaii about 1882 from Nevada, he
launched the *Daily Hawaiian*, and was later associated with
Gibson and Hayselden in the *Elele Poakolu* and *Pacific
Commercial Advertiser*. *Pacific Commercial Advertiser*,
July 15, 1895.

FRI., JULY 1 — *Fred returned from beach this morning.
Whilst we were talking together in the parlor about
10 A.M., Col Ashford entered and ordered us peremptorily
to put on our hats and go with him. A detachment of rifles
in the yard marched us off to the Pac. Nav. Co. warehouse
— an evident purpose to hang us. My anxiety about a note
of M. — managed to chew and swallow it. The pressure
relieved by attitude of for. repres°.*

Talula arrived — pushed her way through the guard —

the brave child. The Com[mittee] of 13 release us. We are marched back to the house. Soon after, arrested on a charge of embezzlement. Marched to police station. Allowed to return to house and remain there under guard.

JULY 1. *Attitude of foreign representatives.* About noon the king met with the U.S., British, French, Portuguese, and Japanese ministers. They advised him to yield to the demands of the revolutionists. Among these demands were the dismissal of Gibson from all his offices, and the formation of a new cabinet under one of certain named persons. The foreign representatives then went to the central part of the city, told the people that a new cabinet was being formed with W. L. Green as premier, and that there was no need for further agitation. R. S. Kuykendall, *The Hawaiian Kingdom, 1874–1893,* p. 364.

Committee of Thirteen, the executive committee of the Hawaiian League.

Arrested on a charge of embezzlement. The guard remained around the Gibson house until the afternoon of July 2. A rumor on July 5 that Gibson and Kalakaua were preparing a coup caused some excitement. The Rifles removed Gibson and Hayselden (both had been charged with embezzlement) to Oahu jail. They were arraigned on the morning of the 6th, and the case was continued to the 11th. On the evening of the 11th Attorney General C. W. Ashford moved for a *nolle-prosequi* because examination of accounts of both men had failed to turn up any evidence to back up the charges. Both men were freed. R. S. Kuykendall, *The Hawaiian Kingdom, 1874–1893,* pp. 365–366.

TUES., JULY 12 — *A good night's rest. The dear Mother and Sister Crescentia came before breakfast. Gift of prayer book and a comforter, and the assurances of faithful, pure affection.*

Fred, Talula & children came — also Fanny and Edith.

*The real affection of Fanny. Goodby [e] to my darlings
— Talula, Walter, Lucy, Dada, Aupuni and the precious
little Rachel. Affectionate words with Fred.*

*At about 12.15 P.M. carriage sent by Wm. G. Irwin
arrived. In company with Mr Neumann drove to O.S.S.
wharf — found the J. D. Spreckels ready to sail — got
on board. The moorings cast loose — and the barkentine
with sails all set sped on her way. Pleasant adieux to
pilot Babcock. Welcome of Capt Friis on board.*

JULY 12. *Capt. Charles S. Friis* of the *J. D. Spreckels,* a
sailing ship of the Oceanic Steamship Co. named for
Claus Spreckels' oldest son John. The ship was headed
for San Francisco.

Capt. William Babcock, government pilot for Honolulu
harbor.

SAT., AUG. 6 — *Foggy and cold in the bay. By 9 A.M.
alongside the wharf. We were expected — reporters after
me. I got into a carriage. Stopped to see Consul McKinley,
and then went to Occidental Hotel.*

*Went out to see Mr A. P. Everett to see about draft &c.
Miserably cold in the streets. Met and importuned by
reporters in the streets — talking, walking and completely
exhausted. Quite prostrate on return to the Hotel.*

*Mr and Mrs Herbert called. McKinley called. So very
cold — had a fire made in my room. Buckland called.*

AUG. 6. *David A. McKinley,* Hawaiian consul general, San
Francisco. He had served as U.S. consul, Honolulu. He was

164

the oldest brother of President William McKinley who was
then U.S. representative from Ohio. Charles S. Olcott,
William McKinley (Boston, 1916), vol. 1, pp. 6–7.

Occidental Hotel, on Montgomery Street between Bush and
Sutter. *Pacific Coast Diary, 1886 and 1887* (San Francisco),
p. 14.

A. P. Everett, commission merchant, 405 Front Street,
San Francisco. McKenney's *Pacific Coast Directory,
1883–1884* (San Francisco). He had also been a
commission merchant in Honolulu.

Mr. and Mrs. Allan Herbert. He was a horticulturist
(specializing in viticulture) at Honolulu's Kapiolani Park.
He and his wife were visiting in San Francisco, and
returned to Honolulu Aug. 23. McKenney's *Hawaiian
Directory*, 1884; *Pacific Commercial Advertiser*, Aug. 29,
1887.

Charles R. Buckland, editor of the *San Francisco Merchant*,
and San Francisco agent for the New Zealand
government. He had been a journalist in Honolulu. In
November 1886, Gibson had asked Consul General
McKinley to discharge Buckland from his position as
Hawaiian vice consul, San Francisco, because of his
friendship with Spreckels. *Hawaiian Gazette*, Feb. 16,
1886; *Pacific Commercial Advertiser*, Dec. 16, 1886, Aug.
29, 1887; Gibson to McKinley, Nov. 22, 1886, Hawaiian
Consulate S.F., Archives of Hawaii.

SUN., AUG. 7 — *My voice gone this morning — hoarse —
inaudible. Suffered dreadfully yesterday.*

WED., AUG. 10 — *Went to St Mary's Hospital.*

AUG. 10. *St. Mary's Hospital*, on Rincon Hill at First and
   Bryant streets, was completed in 1861. Our Lady of
   Mercy School was built on the premises in 1871, a home
   for the aged in 1872, and a new chapel in 1879. The
   hospital complex, well known as the motherhouse and
   novitiate of the Sisters of Mercy, was destroyed in the
   earthquake and fire of 1906. Gibson had a third-story
   private room with a view of San Francisco Bay. Edward

Topham, *St. Mary's Hospital and the Sisters of Mercy,
1903–1949* (privately printed: San Francisco, 1950), pp.
9–13; Sister M. Aurelia McArdle, *California's Pioneer
Sister of Mercy: Mother Mary Baptist Russell, 1829–1898*
(Academy Library Guild: Fresno, Calif., 1954), pp. 60–75.

[No diary entry, but]

SEPT. 23. Affidavit of Gibson in connection with the
breach of promise suit: "... since the 10th day of August
have been an inmate of; a patient and undergoing
treatment as such at St. Mary's Hospital. ... Since my
arrival ... I have been operated upon by Dr. Geo. H.
Powers [for removal of nasal polyps] and have been
continuously attended by Dr. Luke Robinson who has
given as his diagnosis that I am suffering from Chronic
Bronchial Catarrh coupled with a diseased condition of
the left lung. My said malady has so affected me, that I
was unable i. e., physically incapable of making any
deposition in this matter without great danger of
further serious aggravation of my illness and under the
advice of my said physician I have declined to do so. My
physician has advised me that any worry excitement anxiety
or exertion on my part was very liable to bring about a
fatal result. By reason of the premises I am unable at
this time to return to the Hawaiian Islands. It was my
intention to return ... on the steamer which is to leave
for that destination on this day, but I have been
compelled to abandon my intention ... for the present."
Law 2501, Archives of Hawaii.

SUN., OCT. 2 — *Attended Mass 7.15 A.M.*

> *The cough unchecked.*

> *Annie with her three children called.*

WED., OCT. 5 — *When out today, surprised to meet Stilwell
on the street. He said that Dr Trousseau allowed him to
leave the country about two weeks after I left. This if
known would be regarded as an outrage here — that a
man, a confirmed leper, who has been in the Branch
Leper Hospital for four years, should be allowed by public*

authority to depart and inflict his diseased body upon this
community.

OCT. 5. *Charles M. Stillwell*, a carpenter, was discharged
   from the Kakaako Branch Hospital on July 30, 1887,
   presumably as cured. He had been there since Jan. 8, 1883.
   Inmates of Branch Hospital, Kakaako, Archives of Hawaii.

THURS., OCT. 6 — *Arrival of the* Australia — *letters from*
Fred, Talula, children, Walker, and Lyons.
   A letter from the King handed to me by Dr Kuehn.

OCT. 6. *Rolando Kuehn*, appointed in September 1887 ship's
   physician on the steamer *Australia*, which was on the
   San Francisco-Honolulu run. He had been ship's physician
   on the *Mariposa* and Hawaiian government physician at
   Lahaina, Maui, and for the island of Molokai. *Hawaiian*
   Gazette, Aug. 31, 1886; *Daily Bulletin*, Mar. 15, Sept. 27,
   1887; *Pacific Commercial Advertiser*, Oct. 3, 1887.

SUN., OCT. 9 — *A good night's rest. Feeling much improved*
— an easy, comfortable feeling all day.
   Dr Kuehn spent an hour with me.

MON., OCT. 10 — *Had a good night's rest — cough much*
moderated. The improvement in health may be owing
only to the exceedingly pleasant warm weather.
   Wrote letters to Talula, Walter, Lucy, Dada and
Aupuni — to Mother Marianne, J. S. Walker, D. Lyons,
W. J. Roche, Fanny Bickerton — and to the King.

Purchased pair of English pheasants, and pair of carrier pigeons — shipped on board Australia. *Sent to Walter, care of Fanny B.*

OCT. 10. *Improvement in health.* But Luke Robinson, visiting physician to St. Mary's Hospital, certified on this date (in connection with the breach of promise suit) "that Hon Walter M. Gibson is under my professional care, and that I deem it extremely dangerous to have him removed from the hospital in his present state." Law 2501, Archives of Hawaii.

Other affidavits were filed in the breach of promise case, presumably having a bearing on whether Gibson could return to testify. (He did not return.) For example, affidavit by Henry Waterhouse, dated Oct. 19: "I arrived in San Francisco on the first day of October 1887. I know Walter M. Gibson. I first saw him in San Francisco about four days after my arrival. I again saw him on the 10th day of October on Kearney street. . . . Saw him walking very fast and hailing at a street car. . . . Then he came across to the same side of the street I was and walked on the side-walk about five feet ahead of me. He was looking in much better health than when I last saw him at Honolulu. . . . Consul McKinley told me he (Gibson) called at his office nearly every other day. . . ." Law 2501, Archives of Hawaii.

TUES., OCT. 11 — *Departure of the* Australia. *Gave all my letters to Dr Kuehn.*

SUN., OCT. 16 — *In doors all day. A remarkable heavy fog. Looking out of my room windows at 7 A.M., actually could not see houses on the other side of First and Bryant Streets.*

OCT. 16. *Looking out.* From his third floor private corner room at St. Mary's, Gibson could look out on the

residential area to the east, and on South Beach and San
Francisco Bay.

MON., OCT. 17 — *Attended a requiem mass in the chapel at
7.30 A.M.*

WED., NOV. 2 — *Arrival of the* Australia. *Dr Kuehn called on
me. Letters from Fred, Talula and children.*
The infernal suit goes on.

NOV. 2. *Suit goes on.* It was already over. See note to diary
entry for Nov. 17, 1887.

THURS., NOV. 3 — *Letter from M. to care of McKinley.*

SUN., NOV. 6 — *Bought for Lucy a gold bangle — also for
Rachel a gold bangle — for Dada a watch, a real time
keeper — for Aupuni a small music box — for Henry and
Jesse fine pocket knives, and sent a new pair of boots for
Henry.*

NOV. 6. *Henry*, Gibson's son, and *Jesse Morehead*, Gibson's
nephew. See note to diary entry for Aug. 23, 1886. *Lanai
election discussion.*

MON., NOV. 7 — *Mrs Williams recopying the Ms. of last
week.*
Paid Cap[t] Curtins bill of detective bill of $116.00.

NOV. 7. *Mrs. Williams recopying the MS.* It was later reported
that Gibson was writing a book on Hawaiian history,
including the revolution of 1887. "It is given out that
[he] intends dropping a large-sized bombshell into the
camp of his enemies." *Pacific Commercial Advertiser,*
Jan. 3, 1888, citing *San Francisco Examiner,* Dec. 15, 1887.

Capt. Curtins' detective bill. Doubtless for investigating
Mrs. St. Clair's background with regard to the breach
of promise suit.

TUES., NOV. 8 — *The profession of Sisters M. Mercedes and*
M. Agnes — a most impressive ceremony. Sister Rafael
conducted me to an excellent seat for observation of the
ceremony in the organ loft.

    Departure of the Australia. *Gave package for Walker*
to Dr Kuehn. It contained letter to Fred, Talula, Walter,
Lucy, Dada, Aupuni and Rachel.

    Sent presents by Dr Kuehn.

NOV. 8. *Sister M. Mercedes Coleman* left the community
Dec. 30, 1898.

Sister M. Agnes Quinlan (1865–1926) had been in the
"Mater," a home adjoining St. Mary's Hospital, before
entering the novitiate. The home, run by the Sisters of
Mercy for young women seeking employment, offered
technical education. Sister Agnes helped move patients
from the hospital during the 1906 earthquake and fire.

Sister M. Raphael McCormick (d. Apr. 19, 1901) entered
the convent of St. Mary's at twenty-four and spent twenty
years caring for women patients at the hospital. "Sketches
of Our Deceased Sisters" (Sisters of Mercy, Russell
College, Burlingame, Calif.).

WED., NOV. 9 — *Sister Rafael accompanied me to visit the novitiate parlor, and to the Home for aged and infirm females.*

A delightful visit at the novitiate. Very much interested in seeing and talking with the curious old characters of the Home. Sister Mary Thomas a most interesting character. Very much pleased with the welcome of Sister Ambrose.

———

NOV. 9. *Home for aged and infirm females,* built in 1872, became inadequate and about 1881 a new one was built at the corner of Masonic and Turk streets. Sister M. Aurelia McArdle, *California's Pioneer Sister of Mercy: Mother Mary Baptist Russell, 1829–1898,* pp. 70, 124–127.

Sister M. Thomas Duggan, professed in 1882, left the community in 1889 to join the Good Shepherd nuns in St. Louis. "Annals of the Sisters of Mercy" (San Francisco), vol. 2, p. 14.

Sister M. Ambrose Fleming (1855–1889) entered the Convent of the Sisters of Mercy at the age of twenty-one. Caring for the aged was her duty during the last few years of her life. Mother Mary Baptist Russell, a sister of Lord Chief Justice Russell of England, said of Sister Ambrose: "She was young in years (34) and in religion (13) but I verily believe old in virtue." "Sketches of Our Deceased Sisters."

———

THURS., NOV. 10 — *Took a ride out on cars on Market and Kearney Sts.*

MON., NOV. 14 — *Engaged an open buggy or barouche, and drove out to the Presidio barracks.*

TUES., NOV. 15 — *Drove out in buggy to Golden Gate Park and Cliff House. Visited the Sutro Garden.*

WED., NOV. 16 — *Drove about in town. Bought some religious pictures at Diepenbrock Bros. & Doeing's, 1390 Market St. Mailed to Honolulu — to M.*

A small vase for the Novitiate. Caused much pleasant comment and praise. An article of fine Bohemian ware, of very elegant pattern — cost $10.

NOV. 16. *Diepenbrock Bros. & Doeing,* job printers and publishers. Melchior and Franz J. Diepenbrock and Carl A. Doeing. Letter, Sister of Mercy M. Marcella, Burlingame, Calif., to G. Barrett, Sept. 17, 1970.

THURS., NOV. 17 — *News of the verdict against me in the breach of promise suit, by the* Consuelo. *It only rouses me up — stiffens me — and does not depress me.*

NOV. 17. *Verdict in breach of promise suit.* Detailed reports in *Hawaiian Gazette,* Nov. 1, 1887; *Daily Bulletin,* Oct. 28, 29, 1887. Mrs. St. Clair was awarded damages of $10,000. She settled for $8,000 when the defense agreed to withdraw a notice of appeal. It is highly doubtful, in the political climate of the time, that the case was fairly tried. No Hawaiians served on the jury, and some jurymen were members of the Hawaiian League!

FRI., NOV. 18 — *Arrival of the* Alameda — *fuller particulars of the breach &c case. A sweet, noble, inspiring letter from M. It has made me feel very happy.*

SUN., NOV. 27 — *Drove out to the Golden Gate Park — and*

*to the statue of liberty erected by Sutro. It seems to be
a mere plaster of Paris cast.*

TUES., NOV. 29 — *Arrival of the* Australia.
    *McKinley sent me letters from Walker and M. How
happy the letter of the latter has made me — a faithful
loving soul.*

WED., NOV. 30 — *Storming all day — remained in doors.*

THURS., DEC. 1 — *Very stormy, windy and rainy —
remained in doors all day.*
    *Dr Kuehn called upon me, and brought letters from
Talula, Fred, and the children.*

FRI., DEC. 2 — *Visited the Convent of our Lady of Lourdes
in East Oakland. Beautiful Sister M. Nolasco — in charge.
Revd Mother Angela called on me this afternoon.*

DEC. 2. *Sister M. Nolasco Coghlan (d.* Feb. 9, 1912), local
    superior of the East Oakland Convent. She also served
    several terms as mistress of novices, and was once in
    charge of St. Catherine's Home in San Francisco. "Sketches
    of Our Deceased Sisters."

Sister M. Angela Synott (d. Apr. 20, 1909), presided as
    mother superior from 1885 to 1888. She suffered, as did
    Gibson, from attacks of bronchial trouble. Sister M.
    Aurelia [McArdle], *California's Pioneer Sister of Mercy:
    Mother Mary Baptist Russell, 1829–1898,* p. 185. "Sketches
    of Our Deceased Sisters."

WED., DEC. 7 — *Departure of the* Australia. *Sent letters by
Dr Kuehn.*

SUN., DEC. 11 — *Suffering very much all day. A short drive in the afternoon, but suffered very much with cold and aches.*

I am afraid that rheumatism is taking hold. Agonies in my back — twisting, squirming and groaning all the time.

Fire broke out about 7 P.M. in The Little Grotto of Lourdes. A long time before a supply of water could be obtained — and so the flames took possession of the grotto, the school building and the chapel. I was out in all the excitement, and my back agonizing me at the time. I was sorely anxious about my private papers, and ready to move them at any time.

DEC. 11. *Fire in The Little Grotto of Lourdes.* "Just as we returned to the Chapel from supper, a fire was discovered in the small chapel . . . which adjoins our principal one attached to the hospital. Immediately the alarm was given . . . but the supply of water gave out owing to the pipes . . . being too small and there not being sufficient pressure. The firemen had to get water from the bay and this of course entailed time & labor. For awhile it seemed as though the whole block would be consumed so rapidly did the flames spread. The school building, which was to the north of the Lourdes' chapel took fire shortly after the alarm was sounded and it being a one story frame, on the very top of the hill and a high wind blowing . . . the flames made quick work of it. . . . But thank God only one corner of the main chapel was burned. Our grand new organ which had only been used a few times & cost over two thousand dollars, was very much injured from water. We have every reason to thank God that no more damage was done — that it did not reach the Hospital and Old Peoples' Home. "Annals of the Sisters of Mercy," pp. 64–65. See also *Daily Alta California*, Dec. 12, 1887.

174

MON., DEC. 12 — *Passed a painful, sleepless night. So much aroused by all the circumstances of the fire. Glad that the disaster is so much less than there was reason for a while to expect. The chapel will soon be restored and the Sisters will have all put to rights very soon.*

What a glorious company of sweet, good women they are. The Catholic religious woman is a true woman and the best of women — blessed I sincerely feel. How I reverence and love my Franciscans, and these Sisters of Mercy.

TUES., DEC. 13 — *Much cough and tightness in my chest. Caught cold at Presentation Convent — and the events of the fire have disturbed me — and set me back.*

DEC. 13. *Presentation Convent.* Probably Presentation Sisters Convent at Powell and Lombard streets. Letter, Sister of Mercy M. Marcella, Burlingame, Calif., to G. W. Barrett, Sept. 17, 1970.

WED., DEC. 14 — *Suffering very much — agonizing pains in back — tightness of chest — sore all over — and constant cough.*

THURS., DEC. 15 — *Dr Robinson administered hypodermic injection of morphine, to relieve acute pains in my back. Got relief.*

DEC. 15. *Dr. Luke Robinson* (1842–1897), visiting senior physician, St. Mary's Hospital. He was a member of the

Royal College of Physicians (England), a member of the first board of medical examiners for northern California (1876), president of the California Academy of Medicine (1891–1893). J. Marion Read, *A History of the California Academy of Medicine* (San Francisco, 1930), pp. 55–57, 137, 162. See also diary note for Oct. 10, 1887.

FRI., DEC. 16 — *Very prostrate — no appetite — no sleep. Sat up all last night. Swelling of my feet.*

SAT., DEC. 17 — *Last night — most painful and wearisome. My feet very much swollen. Could not put on my boots. Depressed on account of this swelling.*

SUN., DEC. 18 — *The nurse Maggie rubbed my feet well with oil last night. Some diminution of swelling of feet.*

MON., DEC. 19 — *More rubbing, and more improvement of the feet.*

TUES., DEC. 20 — *Still depressed — no appetite — and very little rest.*

WED., DEC. 21 — *Continued depressed tone of health.*

SAT., DEC. 24 — *Arrival of the* Mariposa — *satisfactory news from home.*

SUN., DEC. 25 — *A dull heavy day. Yet there seems to be an improvement in the tone of my health.*

MON., DEC. 26 — *The improvement in health continues.*

TUES., DEC. 27 — *My appetite is returning to me. Moore*

brought me a brace of snipe, which the Sister had cooked for me. Eat them with a relish.

DEC. 27. *Eat them*. Doubtless intended as past tense and pronounced "et."

WED., DEC. 28 — *I purchased another brace of snipe. Eat with continued relish.*

THURS., DEC. 29 — *The arrival of the* Australia. *Dr Kuehn brings me letters from the Islands. News — the King expected to take a stand against the Reform Party — but doubtful.*

Delightful letter from M.

DEC. 29. *The king expected to take a stand against Reform Party — but doubtful*. Here Gibson probably underestimated Kalakaua. Though the king's power had been reduced by the "Bayonet Constitution" of 1887, he made skillful use of his veto power. He also took advantage of dissension among the reformers. See R. S. Kuykendall, *The Hawaiian Kingdom, 1874–1893*, chaps. 16, 17.

Note, however, that on this same day Gibson was reported as being surprised at the boldness of Kalakaua's vetoes, which "show that there is now a sustaining power behind him." *Pacific Commercial Advertiser*, Jan. 16, 1888, citing interview in *San Francisco Call*, Dec. 29, 1887.

FRI., DEC. 30 — *Moore obtained for me today some reed birds.*

SAT., DEC. 31 — *The improvement in my health continues. Very cold.*

Last Days

IN AN INTERVIEW published in the *San Francisco Call* on December 29, 1887, a reporter asked Gibson if he contemplated going back to the islands.

"Yes, that is my desire," he said, "but my friends advise me to remain here and get a good rest first, and they will keep me well informed of Hawaiian affairs."[1] He said the reformers had turned plunderers, that the cabinet was not acceptable to the Hawaiian people and they would welcome a change. He would return to Honolulu, he hinted, to take hold again of the helm of state.[2]

General William H. Dimond of a San Francisco sugar firm, who had good knowledge of Hawaiian affairs, said in an interview with the *San Francisco Examiner* that Gibson dared not return to Honolulu because "he would promptly be run on the reef" (thrown in jail).[3]

Through the first week of January the apparent improvement in Gibson's health continued. He was up and about at times, and went for short drives around town. The newspapers reported many rumors that he planned to go back to Honolulu and regain power. Sometime around January 8, during a sudden cold spell in San Francisco, Gibson took off his overcoat on going to a photographer to have his picture taken. He caught cold and had to stay in bed at St. Mary's Hospital. Though there were some periods of improvement, he began to fail rapidly.[4]

1. Cited in *Pacific Commercial Advertiser*, Jan. 11, 1888.
2. "San Francisco Letter," *Hawaiian Gazette* Supplement, Jan. 17, 1888.
3. *Hawaiian Gazette*, Jan. 31, 1888, citing *San Francisco Examiner*, n.d.
4. *New York Daily Tribune*, Jan. 23, 1888; "Annals of the Sisters of

On January 20 he received many letters from Honolulu "begging him to return home soon and rejoicing at his improved health." He died suddenly the next day, Saturday, at four-thirty in the afternoon. The cause of death was reported as consumption, though the immediate cause was given out as "pneumonia and pleurisy combined." [5] Present at the deathbed were George E. Gresley Jackson, once the admiral of the Hawaiian navy, and F. L. Clarke, a former resident of Honolulu who had been lecturing in San Francisco on such subjects as Hawaiian volcanoes. Gibson's last intelligible word was "Hawaii." [6]

The reverend mother at St. Mary's said that she thought she had never met "a more estimable man nor one so well informed on every subject." [7] Many newspapers across the United States carried long obituaries. The *Deseret Evening News* of Salt Lake City called him "an extraordinary character" whose life was stranger than fiction. His "record is tinged with the hue of romance. Some of its chapters are covered with blots, but the volume is finished." [8]

The *Boston Evening Transcript* said: "He was versatile, thoroughly well educated, a linguist, a scientist, and far superior to any person in the Hawaiian Kingdom. The king made him prime minister and he more than answered the king's expectations. He proved unscrupulous, active, suggestive, and industrious." [9]

The *Daily Alta California* of San Francisco said: "With all his peculiar characteristics, good and bad, he was considered by those who knew him intimately a very remarkable man indeed." [10]

Under the headline "A Life Full of Adventure, Peril and Vicissitude," the *New York Times* said his death "ended a career which rivaled in interest many of those conceived in the fertile brains of the romancers." [11]

Mercy" (San Francisco), vol. 2, 1881–1920, pp. 71–73; *Hawaiian Gazette*, Feb. 14, 1888; *Pacific Commercial Advertiser*, Feb. 9, 1888.

5. "Annals of the Sisters of Mercy" (San Francisco), pp. 71–73.
6. "Coast Jottings," *Daily Bulletin*, Feb. 8, 1888; *Daily Alta California*, Jan. 23, 1888; *Pacific Commercial Advertiser*, Feb. 9, 1888.
7. "Annals of the Sisters of Mercy" (San Francisco), pp. 71–73.
8. *Deseret Evening News*, Jan. 23, 1888.
9. *Boston Evening Transcript*, Jan. 23, 1888.
10. *Daily Alta California*, Jan. 23, 1888.
11. *New York Times*, Jan. 24, 1888.

A requiem high mass for the repose of Gibson's soul was sung on January 22 at St. Mary's Cathedral. The body was embalmed for return to Honolulu on the *Zealandia*, to sail on February 10.[12]

News of the death reached Honolulu by the *Australia* on February 8. The city's newspapers offered little comment compared with the extensive coverage in the United States. The Honolulu *Daily Bulletin* cited "Coast Jottings" as follows: "Although he was undoubtedly mistaken in his methods and purpose, the fact remains that he gave to their service his best thoughts." [13] The *Pacific Commercial Advertiser* cited the *San Francisco Newsletter:* "Mr. Gibson was an active, sagacious bustling man of the world, possessed of great force of character, and endowed with rich mental resources. Whatever may have been his faults it may be truthfully said of him that that which his hand found to do was done well." [14]

The body arrived at Honolulu on Friday morning, February 17, 1888. A box covered with a Hawaiian flag encased the coffin. Twelve Hawaiians carried it from the wharf to a waiting hearse. Some hundred and fifty members of the *Ahahui Poola* ('Sun Head' Society, or stevedores) and the *Ahahui Opiopio* (Youth Society) drew the hearse to the Gibson residence on King Street off Palace Square. There they took the black, gold-trimmed coffin out of the box and placed it in the center of a large, detached reception room back of the Hawaiian Opera House or Music Hall. In the afternoon the lid of the coffin was removed. The face and chest could be seen through a plate of glass.[15]

Next day from ten in the morning until six in the evening the body lay in state. Kahili bearers stood at each side of the bier. Flowers were placed at the head and foot. The Sisters of Charity from Kakaako stood watch while a stream of mourners flowed by. Hawaiians outnumbered all others.[16]

As Judge Sanford B. Dole was leaving the nearby *Aliiolani Hale* or Government Building, he said to his brother George and to

---

12. *Daily Alta California*, Jan. 24, 1888; "Annals of the Sisters of Mercy" (San Francisco), pp. 71–73.

13. *Daily Bulletin*, Feb. 8, 1888.

14. *Pacific Commercial Advertiser*, Feb. 20, 1888.

15. *Pacific Commercial Advertiser*, Feb. 18, 1888; *Hawaiian Gazette*, Feb. 21, 1888; *Daily Bulletin*, Feb. 17, 1888.

16. *Daily Bulletin*, Feb. 18, 1888.

Lorrin A. Thurston: "Well, shall we go and see old Gibson?" They joined the crowd moving past the coffin. Thurston was shocked to see that the embalming fluid had turned the skin very dark, contrasting with the white hair and beard.

Out on the street, Judge Dole asked: "What do you think of it?"

His brother George said after a few seconds' pause: "Well, I think his complexion is approximating the color of his soul." [17]

Long before the appointed hour of a quarter to three on the day of the funeral, Sunday, February 19, crowds gathered both at the Gibson home and at the Catholic cathedral on Fort Street. Father Leonor held a short service at the room where the body lay in state. He then led a procession west on King Street and north on Fort Street to the cathedral, which was already overflowing. Hermann Koeckemann, the bishop of Olba, and Father Sylvester met the procession at the cathedral entrance. Cross-, incense-, and candle-bearers preceded the coffin up the aisle. The bishop, assisted by Fathers Leonor and Sylvester, conducted the funeral service. He said Gibson had died a Catholic and was entitled to all the rites of the church. He spoke briefly on the theme: "Let him who is without fault among you cast the first stone."

The chief mourners were daughter Talula, her husband Fred Hayselden, and their five children; son Henry Gibson; and nephew Jesse Morehead. The presence of the mother superior (Marianne was not mentioned by name) and the Sisters of Charity was noted.

Among other mourners were: John O. Dominis, governor of Oahu; Jonathan Austin, minister of foreign affairs; George W. Merrill, U.S. minister resident; James H. Wodehouse, British commissioner; A. de Souza Canavarro, Portuguese commissioner; Curtis P. Iaukea, the king's chamberlain; William G. Irwin, partner of sugar king Claus Spreckels; Samuel M. Damon, partner in the Bishop bank; George W. Macfarlane, agent for the Hawaiian loan in London; and Volney V. Ashford of the Honolulu Rifles, who had once proposed to lynch Gibson. Notably absent was King Kalakaua, even though his people exceeded all other mourners.

After the service the procession moved south on Fort Street

17. Lorrin A. Thurston, *Memoirs of the Hawaiian Revolution*, ed. A. Farrell (Honolulu: Advertiser Pub. Co., 1936), p. 80.

from the cathedral, and east on King Street to the Catholic cemetery. About one hundred and thirty Hawaiians drew the hearse slowly, to the strains of the Royal Hawaiian Band which led the procession after the undertaker. Thirty carriages followed the hearse. Hundreds of people walked ahead of and behind the hearse. Spectators crowded both sides of the street along the entire route. Father Leonor conducted the service at the cemetery, where temporary interment took place pending proposed construction of a family vault on Lanai.[18]

The Honolulu *Daily Bulletin* concluded its account of the funeral: "He had his friends and he had his enemies. Let us speak kindly of the dead if our profession of Christianity is anything more than a hollow pretence."

Mother Marianne wrote to her superior: "Indeed our loss is great. . . . It seemed that nothing gave him pleasure but to serve and wait upon us. I have never in all my life seen a man like him. We miss him. He had great plans laid out — what all he was going to do for us if God had spared his life. God alone knows the *Why* of all the great trials and mean persecutions he allowed to come over this poor man." [19]

---

18. Accounts of funeral: *Daily Bulletin*, Feb. 20, 1888; *Pacific Commercial Advertiser*, Feb. 20, 1888; *Hawaiian Gazette*, Feb. 21, 1888. See also "Journal of Sister Leopoldina Burns," St. Anthony's Convent, Syracuse, N.Y., chap. 10, pp. 20–22.

19. Letter, May 5, 1888, cited in L. V. Jacks, *Mother Marianne of Molokai* (New York: Macmillan, 1935), pp. 70–71.

Appendix: Mother Marianne

MOTHER MARIANNE (1836–1918), of the Third Order of St. Francis, devoted the last thirty-five years of her life to the lepers of the Hawaiian Islands. She came to Honolulu in 1883 with six sisters from St. Anthony's Convent, Syracuse, New York.

Mother Marianne (Barbara Kopp) was born in 1836 near Darmstadt, Germany. When she was still an infant her parents emigrated to Utica, New York. She received novitiate training at St. Francis Convent, Syracuse, and was professed in 1863. Early in her religious work she showed qualities of leadership and held a number of administrative posts. In 1877 she became provincial superior at Syracuse, a position she still held when a call came to go to the Hawaiian Islands.

Bishop Hermann Koeckemann and Walter M. Gibson had commissioned Father Leonor of Honolulu to find help for the Hawaiian lepers. After making fruitless application to more than fifty religious sisterhoods, he came to St. Anthony's Convent, Syracuse. From a number of volunteers six sisters were chosen, besides Mother Marianne. It was intended that she would help establish the sisters in the Islands and then return home.

The sisters arrived in Honolulu on November 8, 1883, on the *Mariposa*. Royal carriages took them from the wharf and the bells of the city rang out. But Bishop Koeckemann warned them that they "need expect neither praise nor gratitude, but many crosses and much suffering."

NOTE. This account relies mainly on L. V. Jacks, *Mother Marianne of Molokai* (New York: Macmillan, 1935).

They began work early in 1884 at the Kakaako Branch Leper Hospital on the Honolulu waterfront. This segregated area of rickety buildings surrounded by a fence looked more like a prison than a hospital. Sanitary conditions were appalling; just cleaning up the place was a major chore. The work became even harder when Mother Marianne went with two of the sisters to help open a branch hospital, for non-contagious diseases, at Wailuku, Maui. That done, she left the two sisters and returned to Kakaako. She and the four sisters there had charge of more than two hundred lepers.

King Kalakaua noted in his speech to the 1884 legislature: "I am very hopeful of increased health in My Kingdom, and an improved sanitary condition of the country, owing in part to the ministrations of the Sisters of St. Francis."

In a letter to Syracuse in early 1885, Bishop Koeckemann wrote that the continued presence of Mother Marianne was "quite necessary" to the success of the sisters. He praised her ability to deal with people and circumstances and said she enjoyed "the highest esteem and full confidence of all."

In November 1885, on the second anniversary of the sisters' arrival, the Kapiolani Home for girls not lepers but born of leprous parents was dedicated in the Kakaako complex. Queen Kapiolani herself presented the keys to Mother Marianne. King Kalakaua decorated her with the Royal Order of Kapiolani, established by the king to reward benevolent acts toward his people.

It had been intended that some of the sisters would eventually go to the main leper settlement on the island of Molokai. The bishop discussed this with Mother Marianne in early 1887. The project was delayed by the need to build proper housing and by the political unrest resulting in the revolution of 1887 and the downfall of Gibson. But in November 1888, Mother Marianne and two of the sisters landed at Molokai, taking up quarters at the Bishop Home. Father Damien, the leper priest of Molokai, died of the disease about six months after the sisters arrived. Mother Marianne took pride in carrying on some of the work he had been doing. Even though her burdens were now heavier she did not complain.

Robert Louis Stevenson visited Molokai not long after Father Damien's death. One result of the visit was a poem dedicated to Mother Marianne:

To see the infinite pity of this place,
The mangled limb, the devastated face,
The innocent sufferers smiling at the rod,
A fool were tempted to deny his God.

He sees, and shrinks; but if he look again,
Lo, beauty springing from the breast of pain! —
He marks the sisters on the painful shores,
And even a fool is silent and adores.

There were few distinguished visitors such as Stevenson to brighten the days at Molokai.

On one of her few trips away from Molokai, Mother Marianne in 1892 visited Wailuku, Maui. On her return she wrote: "During my absence, Sister Leopoldina and Sister Elizabeth were alone here [at Molokai] — you may be sure I received a warm welcome on my return home." "Home" was the Molokai settlement. And doubtless one of the reasons for the warm welcome was that there was unending work to be done.

As the twentieth anniversary of her arrival in the islands approached in 1903, she wrote: "I am not well, neither am I sick — but I am growing old and am not able to do as much work as I wish to do — we have to pull hard to keep this cart going. . . . Just now we have 98 women and girls in the [Bishop] home; some very bad cases. Ten are totally blind."

On her eightieth birthday in 1916 she was still at work, but could not do much. She said to Sister Leopoldina: "I wish Sister Benedicta to take my place. . . . She is so self sacrificing and courageous, there is nothing too hard for her. She shrinks from nothing. I know she will be able to continue the work."

Self-sacrificing, courageous, shrinks from nothing — the words could well apply to Mother Marianne herself.

Two years later, on August 9, 1918, she died among the lepers she loved and served. She was buried on Molokai. The inscription on her monument reads in part: "Erected by the people of the Settlement."

Index

not go, 112, 123, 132, 133, 135, 141, 144, 146, 153; new fernery at, 22; nursery at, 148; note sent to Marianne, 24; G telephones, unwell, 129; G sends delicacies, 25; G gives Christmas gifts, 97; G sends tray and dishes, 154; G brings charter for Sisters, 83; Dr. Hoffmann, a leper, at, 48; arrival of Father Damien, 58; music at, 93; decoration of altar at, 135; talk with Alfred Carter at, 143. *See also* Convent; Kapiolani Home; Branch Hospital

Kalakaua Home, 117

Kalakaua, King David (b. 1836; reigned 1874–1891), xv–xvii; meetings, lunches, talks, visits with G, 8–134 *passim;* with G at Honolulu fire, 38; wants G five years more, 47; and G's birthday, 114; talks of burying G in Royal Mausoleum, 135; with queen, calls on G, 136; and G's troubles with Wodehouse, 146–147; calls breach-of-promise suit blackmail, 152; appeal to, by G, 160; letter to G, 167; pleased with news from London, 37; no proposals to Armstrong, 66; and London loan, 66, 68, 70, 71, 72, 79, 95; talks with G about loan bill, 72; accepts loan proposals of Spreckels, 76; dislikes Spreckels' amendment, 77; lunch with Spreckels and legislators, 77; breaks with Spreckels, 78, 79; to send G. Macfarlane to London, 78; Nicaraguan canal scheme, 25; proposes military increase, 24; military and opium projects, 25; opium license affair, 116, 145; purchase of *Advertiser*, 154–155; wants electric light plant, 94; extravagance of, 33, 124; and money for guard, 34; at conference on economy, 47; economy message, 53, 55; and extravagant funeral for Likelike, 124; and queen's trip

abroad, 33, 40, 112, 131; buoyant at election prospects, 8; proposes removal of Whitney, 12; proposes removal of officers, 13; wants no office-holder opposed to G, 14; wants Jackson for reform school, 24; meets Dare, 25; and disharmony of ministers, 26; and H. A. P. Carter, 31, 51, 113; and Gulick, 39; speech discussed in cabinet, 41; suggests F. H. Austin as finance minister, 48; and June 30, 1886, cabinet change, 56, 57; talks with Spreckels about cabinet, 63; may remove Judd and Purvis, 65; and Javanese immigration, 83; wants special session, 119; and Pearl Harbor cession, 123; wants Kapena to resign, 127, 130; urges help for Godfrey, 150; agrees to Gulick for tax collector, 150; will accept radical cabinet, 159; stand against Reform party, 177; audience for Spreckels, 44; visit to Kakaako, 49, 50; meets Rossini, 94; receives Feer, Jr., 27; visits Kapiolani Home, 68; and *Tsukuba*'s failure to salute, 73; does not appear at luau, 109; angry with Likelike, 120; condolences to, on Likelike's death, 121; presents flag to Rifles, 136; receives Earl of Aberdeen, 156; gives luau, G sick, 156; and "Star of Oceania," 50, 92; and *Kaimiloa*, 114, 115, 142, 150; to be king of Polynesia, 117; wants Mahelona to replace Bush, 156; agrees to Poor for Samoa, 157; G's birthday present for, 82, 85; and events of birthday jubilee, 85–90; anniversary of accession, 124; coronation of, xvi; not at G's funeral, 181

Kalaupapa, Molokai, 59

Kalawao, Molokai, 53, 59, 64, 124

Kalua, John W., 51

Kaluahine, James, 150